Light and Easy
DRESSAGE

Light and Easy
DRESSAGE

How to enjoy and succeed at dressage at every level

PENNY HILLSDON

J. A. ALLEN

My once-in-a-lifetime horse, Kashmir.

Frontispiece   'St. George and the Dragon' by Penny Hillsdon

© Penny Hillsdon 2008
First published in Great Britain 2008

ISBN 978 0 85131 930 8

J.A. Allen
Clerkenwell House
Clerkenwell Green
London EC1R 0HT

www.halebooks.com

J. A. Allen is an imprint of Robert Hale Ltd

All photographs © Bob Langrish except those on pages 4, 17 and 18 (top right, bottom left and right) and 241. The photo on page 242 is by a former photographer of the David Broome Event Centre.

British Library Cataloguing in Publication Data
A catalogue record for this book is available from the British Library

Design by Judy Linard
Edited by Jane Lake
Printed in China and arranged by New Era Printing Co. Ltd, Hong Kong

CONTENTS

5   CONTACT

ACKNOWLEDGEMENTS

FIRSTLY I WISH to thank all the students I have taught over the years, all of whom are special and have taught me a lot about dressage! A special thank you to the students who rode for the photographs in the book: Annie, Nessie, Angela, Penny, Richard, Melissa and Audrey. A big thank you to the children Callum, twins Charlie and Connor, Eva and Jo and to Tina Isgoren for helping to organize the day for the photographic session. Much appreciation goes to Bob Langrish for his photographs and his unique way of handling the riders in preparation for the shots. Thanks also to the two gentlemen at Crofton Equestrian Centre for preparing the arena surface and even trimming the grass banks, and to Marissa for generously agreeing to the fun photos in the book and for arranging free use of the outdoor arena with the proprietors of Crofton Equestrian Centre. My thanks also to Audrey for the use of her beautiful arena at her horse farm, Grovehill Barn.

A big kiss goes to the cheeky grey mare for allowing me to ride her for some of the photos included in the book and to her owner, Angela. We call the mare the Hollywood Blonde: she knows how to remember what suits her and forgets whatever she doesn't like; now that's a selective memory! She's a dear horse and very forbearing with us humans, thank goodness, because dressage would be nothing without this wonderful trait of the horse.

Thank you to my trainers of past years such as Pat Manning, Paul Fielder,

Charles Harris, John and Dale Lassetter, and David Hunt, and, last but not least, my childhood dressage instructor, Miss Wickham.

I can never fail to mention in my acknowledgements the horses who have taught me so much about dressage, they all inspire awe and love, especially Stozi (Maestoso Stornella II), the Lipizzaner trained at the Spanish Riding School of Vienna and brought over to Goodwood, England by John and Dale Lassiter. Special horses I have owned are my Hanoverian Grand Prix horse Gustav (Carino III), and my Novice horses Ginny (Kashmir) and Rhea (Mirabeau), both Danish warmbloods.

A big thank you goes to J.A. Allen for persevering with my deadline blips! I am renowned for being late with copy, but it seems I surprised them this time. Thanks also to my publisher Cassandra Campbell for her flair for editing and direction with publishing, and to my editor Jane Lake, who is brilliant at picking up fine details, and last but not least to the designer, Judy Linard, who lifts up the whole presentation of a book. Let me thank the Allen's team; without teamwork no book would ever be published.

Lastly I want to thank my mum for putting up with me during my writing days – although not a horsewoman she still supported my dressage riding – for doing my washing, for cooking my meals, and for being a great support.

I hope you all enjoy reading the book. God bless you all, and many thanks to you, without readers there would be no writers, thank you for giving me the chance to write *Light and Easy Dressage.*

INTRODUCTION

A DECISION ALWAYS has to be made about how to refer to the riders and horses in a book and, without wishing to be discriminative, I decided that the riders would be female and the horses would be male, except in particular cases. For example, in the photograph captions I have obviously given the specific gender of the rider and horse illustrated.

The book focuses on getting the rider started in dressage and includes fast-track methods for training the basics of lateral and collection work that are proven to be safe and complementary to the horse's way of going. It spans the first steps to Medium-level dressage and helps those riders aspiring to improve their dressage whether specifically for the dressage arena or for the dressage phase of eventing. Importantly, it will also help the loving owner who simply wishes to get closer to her horse through the art of dressage riding.

1 DIVINE SENSATIONS

SKILLS THAT APPEAR simple can prove difficult – the beauty of classic lines matching the flow of movement – an elusive perfection. Yet riders feel this white elegance, like cutting through clean, untouched snow beneath the open blue skies. Is dressage a sport or an art? This question has baffled many but, whichever it is, it can never be separated from the basics of good equitation. From century to century, the never-changing ways were imprinted by one generation on another. The wheel can not be recreated.

For many 'dressage' implies the competitive arena but the word simply means 'training', training in the manner of the classical masters and schools, and it is important to remember, therefore, that 'dressage' can, and should, apply to all riders and all horses and ponies no matter what their final goals may be. This is what dressage is about, not just the half-passes, the pirouettes, the fancy movements and the extended trots, dressage is training the horse. It rests on an understanding between man and beast.

The divine sensation is a feeling unique to dressage: a rider experiences a horse swinging through his back in a powerful jubilant way, responding to the rider's every aid; a complete harmonizing and blending between horse and rider that cannot be matched (Figures 1.1a, b and c).

Horses are touchy-feely animals. Dressage is basic, it is about training the basics, and it is basic because we are riding an animal. Forget the glitz, get down to the basics, the polish goes on when the basics are in place, and a horse cannot

Figures 1.1a–c   A rider gets a feeling when a horse swings through his back in beautiful movement. The classical masters called it divine sensation.

be trained to any good standard unless he is happy to work with the rider. For ten years I rode only well-trained dressage horses, but then I started to ride hunters and event horses, and I really felt the difference! These were expensive gorgeous horses, but stiff, unresponsive, resistant, because they had not been taught dressage. The experience reinforced my understanding of what dressage should be about.

- To train suppleness into the physique of the horse so that he becomes comfortable and easy to ride.
- To develop a relationship with the horse.
- To give the horse a good life and to achieve personal goals.

A horse can excel beyond the wildest imagination and I am always surprised by what can be achieved. It just knocks my socks off! I have seen it countless times; horses are wonderful, beautiful creatures with speed, grace, endurance, and elegance. Nature has been generous to the horse, and we want to do justice to this superb creation. There is pure enjoyment intermingled with dressage training, a respect within the horse and rider relationship that is beyond compare. The movement of the horse is expressed in dance. Dressage is the ultimate positive riding; there are so many rewards, it is like being a child in a sweet shop.

Happiness and Love Factors

A happy horse enjoys his dressage, a happy horse makes a happy rider, and the work becomes fun. The horse enjoys being trained, his confidence blooms, and this makes him easier to train – a flow of positive learning spirals upwards. Happiness is an important factor when training dressage, as it is in all learning.

Good dressage requires brains, brawn, and ability but nothing of value exists unless it is combined with enjoyment, enjoyment that should be reflected in the smile on the rider's lips, the glow of contentment on the horse's coat: pure happiness. If happiness is present we can face the discipline of dressage, the precision, the learning and the other demands because the happiness brings us to the truth of dressage. Good quality movement will not be achieved unless the training progresses in a happy way, and the horse's muscles cannot contract and stretch in a proper gymnastic fashion unless he is relaxed. I repeat: only if the horse is relaxed and happy to learn will his muscles become supple and only then will the horse be able to do the gymnastics of dressage that are fundamental to its essential nature. Nothing will be gained by being aggressive, or hitting, or punishing; this is not training, but a painful experience for the horse and destructive to the reputation of caring riders. The horse will have the last word, perhaps of resistance and tension, perhaps of more extreme behaviour. Success does not come from training in such ways but from being compassionate caring riders. We look for the picture of harmony between horse and rider, a picture worth more than a thousand rosettes.

Dressage reveals pretensions, you cannot fake happiness, and a healthy relationship between horse and rider is a visible entity. Those watching are drawn towards it: the expert and the uninitiated, complete beginners and the experienced, all see harmony between horse and rider become manifest, a glow of happiness – like oil paint on canvass, an original impression.

The horse has the scope to offer this unique relationship between man and beast, no other animal has equalled him in this respect (Figure 1.2). He has carried man across continents, to peace treaties, to war, to market, to cultivate the land, and to church on Sundays. Today he brings riders closer to nature, we enjoy this closeness, and we yearn to absorb it into our lives – the touching of the horse's coat gives comfort, a cheery feeling that dispels gloom. Today we yearn to be reunited with nature, there is an awareness of saving the planet, of nurturing the earth and riding brings us closer to this need. We want those special moments between man and his environment, and I hope I can introduce this wholesome practical aspect of dressage into your training. Dressage can impart wisdom and understanding.

Horses are the greatest teachers, they reveal strengths and weaknesses of character and talents, and they reveal understanding about us that can be astounding. They present opportunities to feel the closeness that man can have with other creatures that is beyond explanation. We remind ourselves when we put our foot in the stirrup, 'a happy horse is a happy rider', in other

Figure 1.2   A new unique relationship; my student for many years, Tina helped me look after my mare Rhea.

words, when our horses are happy we are happy, and when we are happy we are relaxed and it is then that everything becomes light and easy (Figures 1.3 a–d).

If you love horses they sense it, and will return that love. Some experts say you can never love a horse like a dog or a cat, for example, and you should never treat a horse with the same love. I disagree. It is true that horses do not walk into houses, or sit on dining chairs waiting for treats to be served up on mother's best china, but seeing that glow of love from the eyes of a horse that loves you will make your heart miss a beat. This feeling is unique.

It is a humbling experience to be *superior* to the *lesser* creature, yet find that the horse leads the way in expressions of love for you. So let me encourage you to be brave enough to love your horse. You might be surprised, you will certainly feel happier, and although it is a topic not covered in equestrian books (and indeed often scorned by experts) there is nothing like loving your horse for achieving good dressage.

I have witnessed a strange phenomenon – I call it the happy coat. This is

Figures 1.3a–d   Happiness, love and fun is important in the relationship between owner and horse. a) Richard and Yes My Lady. This boy is known for his gentle handling of ponies – a gift that should never be overlooked or underrated; b) My love for the Irish horse; c) Mirabeau and I share a happy moment; d) Hacking is fun when shared with friends.

when a horse shows his happiness and love for his owner by his coat shining in a special way: a glow that comes from deep within the horse and cannot be artificially manufactured. If an owner has to leave her horse his coat becomes dull and staring, but the moment she returns it glows with happiness again. This happy coat says, 'I love you. I'm happy you are my owner, and my rider.'

But how do we get such intangible factors as happiness and love into our dressage training? It takes great thought but it can be done, and I discuss the topic in each chapter in different ways, because these factors are so intrinsic to training the concept flows through the whole book.

Happiness training is like the house being built on a solid foundation, and the horse can only be trained if he is happy to be trained. This truth cannot be denied. I remember my first teacher. Her horses thrived, they were healthy, happy animals, and each horse was treated as an individual. This love can nurture and prolong a life; my teacher had a 36-year-old pony who looked no older than ten and was a cheeky little chap who loved to gallop. So be encouraged to develop a deeper and deeper relationship with your horse as you go deeper into dressage, let your feelings for each other bubble up, and seek to nurture happiness.

But do not mistake love for a wishy-washy attitude, for passive ineffective riding, the rider is the senior partner in the horse/rider partnership, and sometimes tough love is required, but we only resort to it if there is no alternative (Figure 1.4). Dressage is technique, thought and love (Figures 1.5a and b). Techniques teach love, and happiness guides the rider towards the right technique to use at the right time.

Figure 1.4 Do not think love is a wishy-washy, sentimental thing, it is a living entity, and sometimes tough love is needed. Young horses can be jittery about aspects of riding that we take for granted. This grey was nervous of being mounted and we ensured we gave plenty of training time to get him over this fear.

Figures 1.5a and b   Check that the tack fits well before getting on, a horse cannot be happy if he is feels pain when he is being ridden.

The bridle should fit well, yet bridle fitting is often overlooked. Check that the browband is not too tight, the bit/s hang in the horse's mouth at the right height (this normally means that the lips are *just* wrinkled at the corners) and that the throatlash is not done up too tightly. With the double bridle, the curb chain should fit snugly into the chin groove and be adjusted so that it is just tight enough to bring the curb bit into play when the curb cheek angle is 45 degrees. It can be a little looser on a horse new to this bridle. I favour using a curb chain cover in a soft material, and you must make doubly sure that the curb chain hooks do not catch in the bradoon.

The saddle should not be positioned too far back, or too near the withers, and the girth must lie smoothly around the horse's belly; any pinching around the girth area can cause pain. To ensure that the skin is not wrinkled beneath the girth, gently lift and pull the horse's forelegs forward to smooth out the wrinkles. Always make sure your girths and numnahs are kept clean. Some horses' skin is so sensitive that they need a fluffy sheath around the girth to prevent rubbing.

Check the fit of your tack before you mount the horse every time but if once you are mounted you have any doubts about the bit/s fitting and being comfortable or if you feel the saddle has slipped back or to one side, dismount, check again and readjust if necessary.

I like to tighten the girth gradually before I mount. When tacking up, tighten the girth a few holes before walking to the arena, and tighten it again before mounting. I generally find this tightens the girth enough, but some horses expand their tummies and then breathe in to slacken off the girth, and so after you have walked around a little check the girth again. These seem like obvious and minor details but they make a difference to the horse. Some horses prefer a snug but not too tight girth, and this is fine. If the rider is sitting level it should not be a problem. After dismounting, run up the stirrups and slacken off the girth before returning to the stable. I often loosen the flash or drop noseband too after dismounting, and when riding I never have it too tight that I cannot feed titbits.

The horse must be comfortable, like an athlete wearing the right trainers; you cannot expect a horse to work well if he is feeling discomfort or pain from any part of his tack. For example, check the fit of your dressage saddle regularly; check the fitting because correct dressage training builds muscles and changes the shape of the horse thus requiring the saddle to be reflocked. I have had students who have joked with me saying, 'We don't know whether to change saddles or change trainers because my horse piled on muscle condition so much.'

We see these components expressed in the horse's joy of movement. This beauty is not restricted to brilliant horses, even the least-able horse can be transformed through good dressage training.

Frustration and Faith

We appreciate quality, dressage is quality, nothing of value happens without this quality stamp – the rider learns to identify good from bad, and it requires experience and sensitivity. But dressage comes in a chicken and egg scenario, and this can be frustrating, but if we are brave enough to face our faults, and determined enough to keep practising, the learning goes beyond the realms of dressage riding to a place we perhaps never thought possible. It is as if dressage takes us to periods of meditation, of deep thinking about our place on this earth, and the relevance of man's authority over all creatures of the world. Sometimes the learning of dressage demands that we just keep going – carrying on carrying on (as soldiers say); and if we use our intelligence and join it to our riding experiences the results fall into place.

This process requires faith. Dressage requires the faith to train towards a picture we have in our minds of excellent work, of the horse moving in a quality way. Feelings cannot be shown, but they feature strongly, they involve quality too, and when we combine these two facets of dressage we promote perseverance and success starts to come. We can feel pleased with ourselves.

I want this book to unfold opportunities for you, for your talents to be released and realized, for you to come closer to your horse and for dressage principles to be embedded in your everyday riding. These principles should not be considered the prerogative of competition riders and the performers from the finest schools of equitation; they can improve the relationship between every rider and horse.

There are no short cuts, there is simply the horse and rider working towards beauty, movement married to compassion, and when we reach this stage we are lifted into an equestrian realm that epitomizes the essence of dressage. So many joys, the highs in dressage are limitless, and I want to share them with you.

Theory is important but alone does not produce good dressage; dedication to hours of practice in the saddle does. But I hope I can bring the theory to life so that you can translate it into practice. I want to get close to you as if I am teaching you in your dressage arena at home. I hope this book will spark ways forwards for better dressage. I am going to try to help you achieve this. Please forgive my shortcomings but remember that nobody can do anything well, including dressage, unless they are brave enough to make mistakes, to recognize them, to correct them, and to progress – and so this is my aim for you.

Let us keep a balance and think about cause and effect every time we ride so that we think like trainers. This attitude will overcome negativity; we take the responsibility to think through our riding – that's bravery. We do not plough on without proper understanding, we do not let a glitch widen into a huge hole, but we think sensibly – we study theory, we put this into practice, and we think through the results. We think with the seat ('feel' travels through the body, the aids are prompted in the brain, and the brain instructs different parts of the body to tell the horse what to do) and the horse responds to these instructions. The backside is important to the rider, otherwise causes and effects could not be identified, and we could not direct the training. All horses move beautifully without the weight of the rider, our job is to remedy the problem of the horse having to carry our weight.

Over the centuries riders have cooed 'easy, easy, steady, steady' to their horses and this steady approach makes sense for horse and rider; we *make haste slowly* in order to break deadlocks. Smile when you ride and let the laughter roll out when you pat your horse in thanks, happy you have done a good job together. When you laugh and are relaxed, confidence wells up.

The Correct Attitude to Training

REWARD RATHER THAN PUNISHMENT

When you train by reward rather than punishment you are looking for ways to praise the horse when he does well rather than correcting him when he does something wrong. They used to say during lessons, 'praise your horse,' and I sometimes wonder why this term disappeared. It meant to physically pat, stroke or scratch, i.e. give thanks to your horse, for doing well. A lesson would never end without the horse being praised.

Today, although people do pat their horses, I like to go further than this and speak my thanks in different ways while I am riding. I might say, 'good boy,' or I might chunter sweet nothings in his ear, or say, '*de brave, de brave,*' a classical term that rings sweetly to a horse's ears. Smile sweetly too and say, 'Oh, you're so handsome, little man.' Horses love you talking sweet nothings; such rewards are the modern way of saying thank you. I encourage you to thank your horse more often, and to avoid punishing him.

Horses are naughty sometimes, but unless they are being wilfully bad, I resist punishing. I ignore it, ride on and wait for the horse to do something good, and then I will make a big fuss of him. Gradually, he figures out he is pretty clever, which will make you smile, because you know it was your direction anyway; he just thinks he has outsmarted you by being good rather than being naughty. You have to think like a naughty schoolboy to ride playful horses, and good dressage horses often have a playful cheeky side to their character. There are times you cannot avoid correction, but never be severe. In these situations I use my voice and growl, or flap-flap with my leg to make a noise rather than to hurt. With a well-trained horse I simply withdraw my praise. He then sulks for a few turns of the arena, thinks, 'Where are my rewards?' figures out he had better be well behaved, and then we see a turn about in manners. None of these practices is new; it is called equestrian tact and is a method that has been lost in the technical age. Today people want everything cut and dried, but riding horses does not work like this because they are not machines but flesh and blood.

A LITTLE PSYCHOLOGY

The stick is an artificial aid, not a means of inflicting pain on the horse. Spurs are not designed to be stuck into the horse's ribs, legs should not nag at his sides like a fishwife, and the bit was not made to jag him in the mouth. You see, the very tack we use can turn into a tortuous tool if we are not careful; it is best to think about our riding and behaviour to avoid these pitfalls. Forceful behaviour is not part of our repertoire, we train by teaching through kindness and techniques – this is part of the joy of dressage, and until a horse is properly trained we avoid confrontation for the following reasons.

1. He must learn to come onto the rider aids from obedience and not from rebellion. Only if absolutely necessary punish a horse, and often a sharp tap with the whip once or a growl with the voice will suffice, because horses naturally wish to please. Few are genuinely nasty; some are mischievous like little children, but if you remind them gently but firmly that you are the boss you will find they respond.

2. Because the horse is stronger than you, if you get into a battle he is going to win. The strength a small pony has in his neck is greater than that of most strong men and so we must learn that we train by technique and not strength.

3. Until the horse is trained to work on the aids he will fight the rider if confronted because he knows he can get away with it, and because he knows no better. If he is disobedient once he is well trained, we correct him by putting him on the aids more, and he will be so well conditioned to this, he will just respond.

Horses think they are pretty cool when they are trained by reward (Figure 1.6). They just love being patted and petted. The horse learns that by being naughty he is punishing himself and, as he is an intelligent animal, he soon figures this out. This advice seems obvious but many riders hardly reward a horse (he has to give a terrific performance before he gets a grudging tiny pat), which is terrible! Can you imagine working with a mean-hearted demanding boss like that? You may know exactly what I am talking about, and may even be thinking about your own boss (I hope not) but you may have experienced meanness at some time in your life, and I am sure you hated it. Just imagine being under this sort of authority: someone who never says thank you, who never teaches you how to do a new job and then yells at you for not getting it right, someone who works you to death. Life can be hell under nagging, mean, abusive bosses and we want to avoid working for them. If such a boss is our lot, we start finding ways to lessen the workload, or to get revenge in some way, such as piling the sugar in the coffee, or accidentally spilling it over his clean white shirt.

Figure 1.6   Rewarding your horse with a treat.

Horses are just like humans in this respect: they do not like being put upon and will find ways to get back at you, so think about the way you ride and avoid being aggressive at all costs.

USING YOUR BRAIN

Use your brain! It is the only part of your body that is superior to the horse's, and it is the only part that is going to help you to ride well. Remember, each part of our anatomy is attached to another and movement in one part affects the other and all aspects of riding, as with every other activity, comes from your brain (yet we often forget it), as do your emotions. In dressage we must learn to control our emotions to make better use of our bodies and brains and this is why it is beneficial to our whole being and is not just a physical exercise. In this respect it could be likened to a martial art.

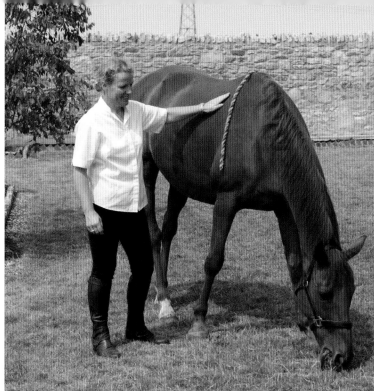

Figure 1.7 (Left)   Take a tip from a student: when you make mistakes say, 'that's pants!'
Carry on learning from your mistakes; we all make mistakes, it is part of the process of
learning. Forgive yourself for making those mistakes and go forward in your work with a
positive attitude.

Figure 1.8 (Right)   T-bags the Thoroughbred taught Audrey dressage.

We are the bosses in the horse/rider partnership and so we have the responsibility of being *good* bosses and being aware of our actions; ignorance is no
excuse. When necessary we reassess a situation and return the next day to use
informed actions. We can make mistakes, but we think them through, and we
have another go (Figure 1.7). *That* is training; it is simple. No doubt, everybody,
in all fields, could benefit from such understanding attitudes and behaviour
patterns, but dressage gives you a real opportunity to do this in a practical
environment. It is easy to do it right.

Do not instil unhappiness. This can happen if the rider has unrealistic
training expectations of the horse: over-facing him, asking him to do higher
levels of competition than he is ready for, pushing him when learning new
exercises or expecting him to be a top performer when he is not. All these

approaches bring unhappiness, but if we temper our expectations we will be fairer to the horse and ourselves, and we will find success and happiness. I have seen it happen many times; believe me, it is a wonderful experience to be the rider that has achieved such results.

We need to be fair, to be just, and we need to understand that all horses can be trained through the lower levels of dressage – and many can teach their riders (Figure 1.8). Even horses not suited to dressage can excel if given the chance but not all horses are going to make it to the national championships, or to Grand Prix. Common sense tells you that it is just not logical to expect it. You cannot plug away beyond the level of a horse's talent, because it brings heartache, and is not fair on the horse. If your expectations are quality Novice and Elementary competition and you train an average horse you will be successful following the training outlined in this book, but if you aim to go higher and are competitive, make sure you have the horse suited to the job.

BACKING: HAPPY TO BEAR A RIDER'S WEIGHT

Imagine being a three-year-old horse and a human you are used to and happy being around has decided it is time you start work. Suddenly objects are plonked on your back, a hard bar stuck in your mouth, something is tightened around your body and the human lands on your back like a predator. A short time ago you were playing in the field, but the fun is soon forgotten as the weight of the human squashes your back and you can hardly breathe because of the pressure around your middle. You are scared; you want to run away, but wherever you go the human is there with you. What do you do? Instinct tells you to gallop off, to buck off the 'predator' and skedaddle back to the field as fast as your four legs can carry you.

The horse feels like he has been put through the wringer. In their natural state horses are happy eating grass, mating, having foals, watching for predators and playing in wide open spaces, but the domesticated horse has to put up with being ridden and having life governed by a human.

This makes us realize just how giving horses' characters are; they lead the way in the generosity stakes – humans cannot compete with them on this score. A person with such a character would be canonised *numero uno* saint instantly, yet 99 per cent of horses are born that way, all little saints in their own ways. Remember this next time you ride a horse. Remember too, that free forward movement is natural to the horse, but carrying the weight of a human being is not. These truths are common sense, but how often do we forget them?

Firstly you have to think like a horse if you want to be a good rider, get inside his brain, and understand that he was born to be wild, to run free, for the wind to blow through his mane and tail, for his hooves to fly over the grass – that wonderful whoosh of energy, the joy of being alive. When that is taken into account and the training progresses steadily, a pleasing phenomenon happens: the rider notices one day that the horse is happy being ridden because he now understands what is required, and he is making efforts to think like a human being (I have experienced this joining of hearts). That is something that will bring a big smile to your lips. Believe me, this will happen if you include happiness factors in your dressage training.

No matter the talent of the rider, if the horse does not want you on his back you are not going to ride him. Teaching the horse to be happy to bear the weight of the rider is the first stage of training, and takes about six months. Yes, you can sit on him from the first moment you bring him in to back him if he trusts you, there is no doubt it can be done, but the point is he has to feel physically comfortable, and he cannot until he has developed the muscle power to hold your weight, to accept your instructions, and to understand rider language. Please do not be in a rush to train this basic stage. It is critical in the horse's development. Backing the correct way allows the horse's muscles to build up gradually. Getting on the horse is easy, but the horse being happy to carry the rider's weight relies upon three aspects:

1. Your attitude to each other.
2. The fact that the horse has developed muscles prior to being backed, i.e. that he has been prepared through work on the ground with long reining, or lungeing, or work in-hand – or all three methods.
3. The rider should know how to 'sit light'. A good rider rides lighter than her natural weight, i.e. supports her own weight, like a dancer, and will make allowances for the undeveloped horse, especially for his back muscles. Also, when she deepens her seat as soon as the horse can accept this, she still

rides light because she goes with the horse's centre of gravity, thus making her weight 'live' with the horse's movement. This makes it more comfortable for the horse to carry her weight.

I have come across horses who have been poorly backed even as seven-year-olds and this has resulted in them not advancing in their training. The only way to clear this blockage is to redo the first backing stage until the horse accepts carrying the rider's weight. If this does not happen he gets tense back muscles, or a cold back (or both), and he is reluctant to work with the rider. These resistances can be traced to the horse's initial backing. The time needed for a horse to accept the weight of the rider in a calm and happy state of mind varies with each horse. It depends on the temperament and natural strength of each horse, as the following examples show.

- A big Danish warmblood I owned took one year to reach this basic stage, but she was so beautiful to ride it was worth all the effort.
- Another big warmblood took one week because she had such a trusting nature, and had obviously been well handled by her previous owner.
- An Irish horse took one month, followed by three months rest to grow, and followed by another two months steady backing work.

Be sensitive to the needs of each horse: the different physiques, different psychological needs, and different learning rates. When backing youngsters a rider should combine her own knowledge and experience with help from experts, but providing common sense is used together with a sympathetic attitude, it is easy to do. If you are inexperienced, or worried you might get it wrong, go to a knowledgeable trainer and work alongside them. There are many such trainers who are good at their work, but try to keep the young horse in his normal environment while he is being backed. It is better that he progresses slowly rather than being sent away for quick backing but if he has to be sent away, I would advise an owner to research the trainer backing her horse, taking into account their reputation, and personal observations. Remember that the horse is special to you but not necessarily special to the person he is going to.

This book does not cover backing youngsters in detail, but I have included some helpful information.

Conclusion

Understanding dressage is the alpha and omega of horsemanship. Riders want to enjoy being with their horses in a healthy working relationship that enhances their time together, they want the best from their dressage, the best knowledge and the best access to trainers. My role in this book is to unravel the mysteries, to open the hidden depths in a way that is easy to understand.

For 500 years dressage had been the preserve of a few; equitation Masters taught privileged students and only tiny drops of this exclusive teaching were spread outside these pockets of excellence. But in 1952 dressage training had become more readily available to the general rider and non-army male riders and women could compete at Olympic and EFI levels. Now all riders have the opportunity to compete, break records and to achieve more than was ever achieved in the past. Now new dimensions to dressage are welling up that blend past knowledge with twenty-first century thinking. Past attitudes of secrecy and exclusivity are blown open, nebulous ideas disappear. A sense of proportion is coming to dressage that makes it accessible to riders all over the world.

2 BALANCED RIDING

WE TREASURE THOSE moments when we watch horses moving at liberty; beauty set in movement, like dance. *If they only moved so beautifully when we ride them,* we think. Capturing this beauty is the purpose of dressage and simplicity is the key. We want clean cut lines and so we must consider our riding position. Does it coordinate with the horse? Does it restrict free forward movement? Does it allow the training to advance? Is it comfortable for horse and rider? The answers lead to truths about our dressage training, and by correcting faults we can improve the horse's way of going.

Riding position is 50 per cent rider balance, and 50 per cent horse balance. The development of the horse's balance through dressage training affects the quality of your position and so it is easier to look good on an advanced horse than on a novice one but to develop the horse's balance, the rider must be able to help the horse. We therefore have another chicken and egg scenario, but if we follow the rules we can overcome such drawbacks. A good way to progress is:

1. To establish your rider position.
2. To sit 'live' with the horse, i.e. to allow the energy to travel unrestricted through the horse's body. But we are flesh and blood, not machines; we are living, breathing entities, each of us has a different body shape and different talents and can therefore only apply rider position rules when we allow for our own individual physiques, otherwise we become stiff and rigid riders.

Put simply, it is impossible to sit stock still when a horse moves, and if we try to force this issue the human body stiffens against the movement. To maintain a quiet position we first have to develop an independent seat, which allows us to absorb the movement through our bodies, and to be in balance with the horse.

3.   To develop rider coordination. This means moving different parts of our bodies at different intensities, while thinking through our riding, and staying fluid with the horse's movement. Most people can ride a horse after a fashion, but in dressage we want to achieve more – quality of movement and a quality relationship – and this prods the rider to muster the dedication to strive for a refined way of riding.

4.   We become increasingly able to marry the different aspects of riding while keeping a good position when we have mastered the basics of developing a good seat. This increases our ability to be good riders/trainers.

Once the horse is suppled his balance becomes refined, and this automatically gives the rider a better position. The ideal situation is for a rider to learn on a horse two steps in advance of her riding standard. This is often not possible, but there are plenty of opportunities to excel if you are sensible, take it slowly, and follow the basic rules.

KISS is an acronym (keep it sweet and simple) that serves as a mnemonic to guide us towards a way of improving that is achievable. Below are the two key parts of riding.

1.   The geometry of the rider's position.

a) Sitting square to axis.

b) The rider's seat.

c) The positioning of other parts of the body.

2.   Rider 'feel'. This is the ability to:

a) apply the aids;

b) be in tune with, and to have an ear for, a horse in the way that a musician has an ear for music; it is a nebulous cloudy entity and the best way to develop it is through correct repetition through informed practice.

Today we watch television programmes like *The X Factor* and often we spot the talent, yet it is not definable, and we sense it, but we cannot explain why. There is an X factor to dressage riding that says that despite everything being against the odds the rider still produces lovely moving horses. Yet often we cannot see why one rider is better than another; we look at the riding position and try to see what is producing such good results. For example, the talented rider may *appear* to have the same riding ability as a less talented one but the difference is demonstrated in their horses' way of going. This is the X factor of riding. It cannot be taught, it is inherent. Nonetheless, in dressage the average rider can get good results if she applies herself to learning. This is another joy of dressage; if you are keen you can achieve success.

The Geometry of the Rider's Position

This covers the proven ways to sit, the lines to follow such as shoulder–hip–heel, elbow–wrist–hand–bit, and give a picture to aim for, an image that sets a standard. We do not want to re-invent the wheel, we want proven rules to work in our favour, yet neither do we want the riding rules to be so rigid that do not allow for individual differences, i.e. of our physical make-up, and we use this information to enhance strengths and diminish weaknesses.

SITTING SQUARE TO AXIS

This is a golden rule of riding. The rider sits level and in balance with the horse's centre of gravity, otherwise all the rider position rules are of no use. The shoulder–hip–heel line puts the rider in an upright classical position, but if it is not applied properly it can cause stiffness. The rider looks at diagrams, sees one side of the rider with a line cutting through shoulder, hip and heel, and aims to copy an immovable picture, but we are not statues. We never ride using just one side of our bodies (we do not unhitch the left side from the right); the centre of gravity runs through the middle of the rider's body not to the side, a principle explained by Maximillian von Weyrother, a nineteenth-century rider at the Spanish Riding School of Vienna, whose directives are still in use at the School today: 'For the rider to be in equilibrium, <u>the line of gravity must fall between</u>

the three points of contact; the trunk should therefore be carried in such a way that the position of all its parts ensures that the line of gravity falls into the rider's base. The distance between these three points, which form the actual support of the trunk, cannot be changed; the seatbones are the lowest ends of the pelvis, and the coccyx is fused with the pelvic girdle via the sacrum…'

This principle complements sitting square to axis because it relates to the rider sitting with the centre of gravity of the horse. When you sit square to axis you stay in balance with the horse's centre of gravity, i.e. ride in balance with the horse.

You may ask: how can I ride a correct circle and remain in balance with the horse; how can I ride straight lines well? To achieve both you must let your shoulders mirror the horse's shoulders, and your hips mirror the horse's hips – that is sitting square to axis.

Look in the direction the horse is going:

1. If the horse is going straight you sit straight, you put equal feel through a live seat and equal weight on both seat bones and equal weight on both stirrups. Your shoulders are level. (When you adjust your position for inside bend you sit the tiniest bit to the inside to encourage inside bend)

2. If the horse is moving on a circle (or any part of a circle such as an arc) look between the horse's ears, and mirror his shoulders and hips with your shoulders and hips. Because his shoulders are pointing along the line of the circle, your shoulders and hips will also point along its line. Sometimes it is easier to think *shoulders and hips follow the same direction as the line of the circle*, the outside shoulder and hip come around together to follow this line of the circle equally. This rule also applies to the inside shoulder and hip coming equally back, so that your upper body and seat are balanced equally with the horse's shoulders but without contorting your body. This effect of your shoulders and hips mirroring the horse's shoulders along the line of movement is a smooth movement and the alteration from sitting straight for straight-line riding and sitting for the line of the circle should not be exaggerated.

When you ride in an arena, the horse moves along a track whether you are riding straight lines or doing circle work.

There are three parts to the track:

1. an outside line
2. a middle space (the area the horse is moving along)
3. an inside line.

It is like children playing trains; they like to build the tracks in different shapes. If a train continues to go straight when it should be travelling on a circular track the train will skid off the track and crash. The effects are not so dramatic when riding, but if you ride a horse on a circle as if he were going along a straight line you unbalance him. Set your sights on the middle of the circular-track lines, keep your body reflecting the shoulders of the horse, look in the direction the horse is moving and you will sit in balance. When a rider sits with the weight unequally distributed, i.e. unlevel, the horse struggles to keep his balance and faults will appear: he will run faster losing the rhythm of his gaits, fall on his forehand, dip his back, grind to a halt (or do all these things) because he has no option, otherwise he will topple over in a heap. Think of your position before you blame the horse for a mistake, many faults can be traced to it. Correct it and feel the difference.

The classical riders knew the truth about position; I quote Charles Harris: 'Square to axis ensures that the rider's shoulders are placed parallel over and above the rider's hips, which ensures that without any twisting and/or distortion of the rider's spine, the rider is in the correct – efficient – vertical posture to use the various stages/degrees of bracing the back to accommodate and absorb changes in tempo, rhythm, cadence, and/or gait variants as required.'

And about the rider's position in circles and changes of directions Charles Harris said, 'Your hips should remain parallel to the horse's hips and your shoulders parallel to the horse's shoulders. You should look in the direction in which you are going. When moving on a curve, a circle or round a corner, the horse should appear to bend his body from poll to tail to comply with the curve on which he is travelling. This is termed bend.' (*The Fundamentals of Riding* Charles Harris, J. A. Allen, 1985.)

THE RIDER'S SEAT

The seat comprises the rider's bottom and hips, but because they are so directly related to the position of the upper body and the thighs, and to some extent the lower legs, the seat is often used to describe the rider's whole position. In fact, we say developing an independent seat is the first stage of riding dressage, and this means all those parts of the body in direct contact with the saddle. I have seen outstanding gold medallists ride with shoddy lower leg positions yet ride with such brilliant seats the results have been spectacular. This is unusual of course but it does prove that if you can ride with a good seat you have got it sussed!

Many riders claim that the only way to get a good seat is to work without stirrups, but I dispute this idea. If a rider has a sound, stable seat then riding without stirrups is easy, otherwise it can cause pain, stiffness, and gripping. I, therefore, tend to get my students riding comfortably with stirrups, and then work them for just small amounts of time without stirrups, either on the lunge or while riding in the arena.

A good way to deepen the seat is to slip your feet out of the stirrups while walking your horse around to warm up. Let them hang down loosely and relax. Now loosen your shoulders by making circular movements with them, and perhaps your arms (one at a time if your horse is well behaved), and if your thighs are a little plump put your hand underneath the mass of the inner thigh from the outside of the leg and lift it up and away from the saddle so that the thigh has a flat surface against the saddle. Walk the horse for five to ten minutes doing these pre-riding exercises and then slip your feet into the stirrups. Now feel your whole body relaxed and, if necessary, loosen and supple any part of your body that still feels stiff. Now you are ready for rising trot, letting your horse come softly up through the back by means of forward active work and, as soon as he does, slide into sitting trot.

In the following text I have discussed the gait seats in the order of trot, canter and walk because it follows the classical concept of riding the horse fully on the aids to the contact in this gait sequence. However, in order to obtain the correct feel for each gait you may prefer to start with the walk seat, progress to the trot seat and finish with the canter seat.

The trot seat

Study the sequence of the trot footfalls (see page 90) and how to recognize the feel of the gait (see page 92). The rider has to learn to 'sit soft' for the sitting trot, i.e. not to be stiff, heavy or aggressive with the seat but to sit live and follow the movement coming through the horse's back. However, if the horse is not working through the back this is difficult, especially for a novice rider, who would, in effect, block the movement from coming through, inducing more stiffness and making it more difficult to sit well and absorb the movement. I advise students to remain in rising trot until the horse is working happily through his back (in training terms this can take from six months to a year) and always to move the seat forward and back into the saddle when rising (not up and down vertically as some riders do) letting the movement through the horse's back push the seat out the saddle for the rise. If you are not sure how to do this take your stirrups away for a very short time and ride rising trot without stirrups, because this will give you the correct feel. People often rise too high losing the closeness with the horse, and it can put them behind the movement.

Assuming all is going well and you are ready to start learning sitting trot, the best way to start is to take rising trot, slip into sitting for a few trot steps, and return to rising trot again. You are focusing on keeping the same rhythm and outline so that the horse is just as happy to bear your weight in sitting as in rising trot. Build up your ability to do this work gradually over a few months, always warming up in rising trot, but starting to use sitting trot in preparation for the collected trot.

There are no exact rules about when to teach sitting trot. I have had students training their horses well into Elementary standard before I ask them to start sitting trot, and others that start at Preliminary stage. It all depends on the needs of each horse, and each rider, but one golden rule is to err on the side of safety, and if you have a big-moving horse stick to rising trot until you are nearly ready to teach collection.

Once the rider can maintain sitting trot I advise short stretches of this work under instruction before they practise alone. However, even this rule can be broken. Some students are competent riders and yet struggle with sitting trot. In this case, they need to just keep doing it until they have mastered it. Once they feel comfortable in sitting trot with stirrups I might suggest some lunge lessons, or starting their lessons with ten minutes lunge instruction.

The canter seat

Study the sequence of the canter footfalls (see page 91) and learn the feel of the gait (see page 93).

The canter footfall sequence is in three-time and your hips follow this movement as it comes through the horse's back. The first step is the first beat of the sequence and is particularly pronounced in walk-to-canter transitions with a feeling of a lowering of the seat as the horse engages the outside hind leg. With the next canter beat the movement travels through and 'up' to what dressage riders call the top of the canter, where the feeling comes up towards the crutch. The third beat comes when the leading leg reaches forward.

Each canter bound gives you this 1-2-3 feeling in your seat as your hips follow the movement and your bottom remains stable, supple and quiet in the saddle. Avoid pushing with the seat but just follow this 1-2-3 movement coming through the horse's back.

The walk seat

Once again, study the sequence of footfalls in the walk (see page 90) and the feel of the gait (see page 92). Once you understand the implications of the horse's steps in walk moving through his body to your seat, you will comprehend the pushing from the horse's quarters that will push you forward toward the pommel of the saddle. Keep your hips supple and they will follow the backward and forward rhythm: forward as the horse steps from his hind legs and backward as the movement comes to meet the pushing of the hind legs again. Avoid tightening you hips against the movement but allow them to flow with the movement (in the same way that a belly dancer allows her hips to remain supple and fluid. Only if you want to collect the walk do you 'close' the seat to neaten the horse's overtracking. But, generally the walk is ridden with the seat in this 'following' supple fluid way that allows the seat to follow the movement of the horse's back as he steps through actively.

Development stages

It is important to understand the stages of development and to consolidate each stage before moving on to the next. Often this involves reviewing previous stages. This is where training exercises on the lunge can be helpful. I explain the three basic stages of riding to my students as follows.

1. To ride in a **workmanlike** way that is effective and good.
2. To ride in a **skilful** way that blends the workmanlike way with the next stage, i.e. to become an equestrian craftsman, an artist.
3. To become **artistic** in riding you reach the higher realms of equestrianism. If you have a strong desire to achieve this and apply yourself to the first two stages – and providing you have a little talent – the preparation work will help you become an artistic rider.

The first two stages are within the realms of most dressage riders, and many advanced riders never take the step from being skilful to artistic, but it is not to say they are not good competition riders. On the contrary, we see some competition riders who are so brilliant they rival even the greatest artistic riders of the classical schools.

Some riders look as if they are having a cup of tea with their granny, and hold the china cup with two fingers. Their riding is too fragile and they have not even established the basics; I encourage them to break away from this misguided idea that dressage is just a matter of looking pretty. You actually have to do something to be a good dressage rider. To achieve the first stage – workmanlike – a rider must be an effective rider and ride in a balanced, harmonious way. What is the purpose of looking pretty yet producing nothing? Why do dressage? You are supposed to be training the horse. We are not models for riding positions, we are riding to improve our horses, and although this requires a correct riding position we should not be obsessed with ourselves. The focus should be on our horses first and then we can build up our riding experience over time. Put some welly into your riding, aim to get results, to train your horse, to improve his way of going – be positive.

Once I feel happy a student has reached this first stage I want to raise the stakes, I want them to move on to the second stage and become really good riders. I focus on them more, on them becoming skilful, to make them beautiful riders. I concentrate on minute details of their position, get them to think through the causes and effects of what they are doing, and maybe give them some lunge lessons. Some schools of thought condone a 'make or break' attitude, getting the rider to do ridiculous contortions to get that elusive riding position. This often includes hours and hours of work without stirrups, and completely sours many a budding dressage rider. In the past, it may have served cavalry officers who had to get fit quickly to ride with a safe seat in preparation for war but we are not riding our horses to war, we are riding them for pleasure and sport.

As already discussed you should **sit with the centre of gravity** and **square to axis**. **Sit on the vertical**, i.e. your upper body must not be in front of or behind the movement. The exceptions to this are: 1. if you are taking the forward seat (see examples below); 2. if you sit behind the vertical, i.e. behind the alignment of shoulder–hip–heel, for a specific purpose, for example in walk to canter to get the upward thrust of the transition, and to ensure you are not tipped forward by the power of this gait.

Ride with the **classical seat** as explained throughout this chapter but if particular situations demand a different approach you can adapt it to suit the needs of your horse.

Different seats and their application

Today, many competitors ride in the classical position, but with adaptations for the modern warmblood horse. They have found that these adaptations make life easier for horse and rider, and include sometimes taking a slight show-jumping forward position when riding young horses, putting more weight into the knee rolls for certain movements with the developed horse in order to free his back muscles, and sitting on, and sometimes behind, the vertical for certain movements. The rider has to be flexible with her own physical make-up, and adapt to the conformation and strength of the horse.

Adopt the **slight forward seat** if a horse stiffens in his back. This can be used for trot and canter. In this slightly forward-positioned seat the weight goes more through the knee into the knee rolls and the seat is lightened. This can be a tiny amount and not easily seen, or a large amount almost like that of a show jumper. You can use this forward seat for particular movements, or for short periods within a schooling session, or for the whole lesson. Check that whatever you do is done for a specific reason, and not just because you cannot ride in the classical position, i.e. the normal dressage position.

Sit on the horse with a **live seat** that allows the energy through and the horse's movement forward; avoid pushing and grinding your seat into the horse's back, because you block the energy coming through and the forward movement. The seat should be relaxed so that you sit in harmony with the rhythm of the gait. Your legs should be soft, embracing the horse gently and not gripping, because this also blocks the energy coming from the horse's hind legs through the body. A dead seat and tight gripping legs resemble the effect of driving a car with the handbrake on – you do not go anywhere! Take the handbrake off and you will feel the energy flowing.

Once you have started collection you begin to develop a **contained seat**. This is a seat that keeps the energy within the frame of the horse. It is difficult to define the contained seat but it is more a lifting up through the ribcage, a feel of up and forward and yet holding the energy moving through the horse's hindquarters. *There is only one way to gain a contained seat and that is to train through collection* but because there are so many degrees of collection, by the time it becomes critical you will automatically have one. Just stay balanced, drive in and drive out of trot-to-halt transitions, ride *good* transitions and half-halts, practise holding the energy on the seat, i.e. through a contained seat. Practise developing a contained seat by riding transitions and eventually you will be able to apply this collecting seat without restricting forward momentum. A good dressage trainer will help you develop the contained seat that is needed for the collected gaits. It is delicate riding but good riding comes through good repetition and riding through collection situations and half-halts fosters an advanced dressage seat – the trainer helps consolidate it more quickly.

Once you have mastered the basic position, you will be hungry to advance; do not worry, it is such a joy to ride and if you get the basics in place first, and then look for a suitable trainer who can teach you this advanced riding, you will never look back because it gives so much more dimension to your communication with the horse. Plus, if you only do a little of this more advanced riding you will benefit, so do not be discouraged. Think of it as a goal to be aimed for at the right time and you will achieve it easily in a natural way.

Today we use the **angled seat.** This is the rider position with the upper body vertical, the thigh pointing towards the knee roll, and the lower leg back towards the girth. It evolved from the show-jumping position invented by Caprilli. In the old hunting prints you see the riders sitting and leaning back and slipping the reins to jump fences, but Caprilli studied the horse's changes of centre of gravity when jumping, and realized that if the rider alters position to follow the horse's centre of gravity as he takes off, goes over, and lands, then the horse can jump better. The modern classical school evolved their own angled seat, taking ideas from Caprilli. Formally they had ridden in the stretched deep seat and we see examples of this rider position in the old paintings of the sixteenth and seventeenth centuries. The cavalry officers sit upright with out-thrust chests, legs hanging down long in saddles with high pommels and cantles, which held the riders in a fixed position in the saddle giving stability and security when riding, particularly in the battlefield. But the stretched position required years of training and there was limited flexibility of the rider's body. The angled seat proved so successful that it has made the stretched seat obsolete.

Think of the maxim 'Mae West east and west' to help you expand the chest and sit taller. If you are not sitting up, ride tall, taller than you actually are and, again, expand and open your chest. When you enter an arena sit up, look elegant and adopt the attitude of the Queen of Sheba; you are important and should be noticed. You might not feel like you are but now you are putting on a show and dressage was created for royalty – so ride like royalty. Never listen to anyone saying that you are no good, believe that you are, sit taller and ride on with grace. Forget what others think, focus on what is happening underneath your seat, focus on your horse, and let the marriage between you both come out into a display that appears beautiful. A large chunk of riding is in the mind, if you think you are good, you will be good – this also applies to your riding position.

THE POSITIONING OF THE OTHER PARTS OF THE BODY

The seat is the rider's base. The upper body and the limbs extend from it. Let me explain the position of the different parts of the body starting at the top.

The head contains the heaviest bone in the human body: the skull, the movement of which can make dramatic changes to a rider's position and weight distribution. You overcome the dangers of looking down and putting weight onto the horse's forehand, for example, by keeping your chin level, the eyes looking ahead and the back of the neck straight. You can look down, with minimal head movement, to check that you are holding your hands correctly, but should reposition the head afterwards, with the eyes looking upwards and the chin level again. Eyes are important; you look in the direction in which you are riding so that the horse's movement can flow easily in that direction. Concentration is so important to good dressage riding and will often show in the face. There will be times when the work goes so well that you want to laugh, smile, or even cry. Relax, this is fine, facial expressions are allowed in dressage; I love my students laughing during lessons it seems to relax then, and I encourage them to tell me jokes while I train them. Sometimes they cry too, but generally with joy at having achieved a movement they thought was beyond their reach. This expression of the emotions is a natural way for a rider to get to know the strengths and weaknesses of her character. It seems to get the poisons out of the system, a sort of dressage irrigation that clears all the nasties out. It works wonders for esteem and for developing a down-to-earth relationship between rider and trainer. It requires trust and this can only be gained by working together over a period of time.

Keep **the shoulders** level so that the seat remains level. Riders find their shoulders get stiff, especially if they work on computers, or lounge in armchairs watching television (all these activities can unravel posture) Stretching exercises help as does checking the shoulders are always held square and level to the body. If they stiffen, lift them up and roll them back and down; feel the rib beneath the breasts and lift the diaphragm up as the shoulders are lifted up and rolled back.

This is a good suppling exercise before riding begins; it can also be done before mounting or when in the saddle.

The arms are attached to the shoulders, and therefore how the rider holds her hands is connected to how she carries her shoulders and can influence the balance of the seat, via the central nervous system. It seems so obvious but it is worth thinking about. Because so many people carry tension in their shoulders, in order to correct the arm position the rider must first supple and relax her shoulders as described above, and then let her upper arm hang down naturally. The elbow is held relaxed near the waist, and the forearms held at about a 45 degree angle to the saddle. However, the angle depends on the length of the rider's arms, the head carriage of the horse, and the tempo he is moving in. For example, the more elevated the gait, the better the self-carriage, the more the rider can keep the shoulders and upper arms in a position that best benefits contact with the bit. A rider must constantly check the upper body is correct or the hands cannot be 'feeling' hands.

Do not rest the weight of the arms or hands on the reins, which is a common fault. To overcome this, imagine carrying a handbag over your arm or holding a glass of champagne; the arm supports the handbag or glass, not vice versa. Keep the tension out of the forearm, and keep the biceps in the upper arm relaxed. Riders are not required to be body-builders!

The **hands** are connected to the bit and can be described as an instrument with which to make music with the horse's mouth. Remember, the horse has a mouth as sensitive as a human being's and it should be treated with respect. Never abuse the mouth by getting rough with the hands. If ever a rider feels she is getting riled up or frustrated she should dismount and calm down or go out for a quiet hack. Never train a horse in anger and never allow aggression to travel to the hands. These practices go against the principles of dressage riding. (Figures 2.1–2.6)

The thumbs are kept uppermost so that the rider can see the little fingers. Avoid 'pram hands' with the thumbs turned down and the knuckles uppermost, but when the thumbs are positioned slightly to the inside it keeps the hand soft.

Figure 2.1 This photo illustrates that in reality you hold the rein with the thumb and forefinger only, the rest of the hand is for closing and opening the rein. This puts the rest of the hand in persective. A quiet hand is the best hand.

Figure 2.2 A good position of the hands, the line flowing through the elbow-wrist-hand-bit is unbroken, and the hand should be soft with the thumbs turned very slightly towards each other. Ride with the thumbs upward if your knuckles stiffen and round spoiling the line to the bit. Hold the reins in an elegant way; the horse likes to feel your presence, and so the feel has to be like a good handshake, neither too wimpish, nor too rugged. The classical school says it is like holding a bag of sweeties at the end of the rein, the horse has to feel, 'Yummy, I like this rider holding the rein, I like the connection.' It is an intimate feeling that expresses the sensitivity of the rider.

If you are still consolidating your seat and hand position, always ride with the thumbs on top of the reins because this helps the important rule of maintaining a straight line of elbow–wrist–hand–bit.

The elbows can be softened to allow the arm to extend towards the horse's mouth in order to give the reins from ½–2 in (1–5 cm) when riding an untrained horse but the hands are kept still. Once the horse is well trained the hands can

Figure 2.3 'Side-rein hands' are held wide apart and low and emulate the side reins. However, like the side reins themselves, the hands in this position can never be as feeling, or react so well to different balances of each gait, and can deaden the horse's sensitivity, so use this hand position with care.

This modern way of holding the reins is often suitable for young horses and when riding the horse long and low, or for horses resisting the contact acting as a stable base. Be careful that you keep the hands steady, and that your position is also steady and with the horse's movement, otherwise this hand position can disconnect the horse's straightness through the shoulder. For this reason I advise you use it for limited periods of time, and for the reasons explained above.

be used in a more refined way. For example: lifting the reins slightly upwards and forwards to encourage self-carriage, and turning the wrist away from the horse's withers gives an open rein and turning it towards the withers gives an indirect rein. (The open and indirect reins are explained in Chapter 5.) The basic rules are: 1) the quieter the hands are the better; 2) the hands are always used in a forward-thinking way from a stable position and they are never drawn back towards the rider's body.

The weight in the reins resembles that of the tension of a piece of stretched elastic, but this weight varies with each horse and his standard of training; generally, the more advanced a horse becomes the lighter the feel becomes. The amount of weight will also fluctuate depending on the exercise being done. You will know there is a problem if the weight feels heavy in your hands, either the horse is not working through actively enough or he has dropped on his forehand. Fluctuations in the contact point will make the balance les stable and this is often solved by riding more forwards, or half-halting to contain the energy.

A horse will use the hands as a fifth leg if you do not ride with the legs and

Figure 2.4 Closing the fingers in a 'squeeze' around the rein so that the contact is taken up a few inches and then releasing this squeeze to give the *give and retake* feel on the rein. This action is often used for the half-halt, although for a novice horse it is better that the action comes through the elbow. The elbow is softened to allow the arm to extend towards the horse's mouth by a few inches. After this softening it returns to the original position. The hands are kept still and the contact remains the same. Once the horse has come through from behind and is yielding in the mouth, i.e. accepts the bit in the mouth, and accepts the half-halting actions of the rider's hands – normally at Novice or Elementary standard, but this depends on the horse – then you can use these tiny give-and-take actions with the hand that will travel through the rein to the bit. The horse's mouth has to be relaxed to accept these actions or he will just stiffen his jaw, the stiffness goes to his poll and travels through his topline blocking the forward energy.

I prefer to use the hands for flexion and direction only until the horse is coming through from behind, and introduce the give-and-take actions on the outside rein to slow the speed. I stop the horse through the seat as explained in this section's text. This ensures free flowing movement and is the classical way to ride.

Figure 2.5 Giving the rein through the hand by three fingers opening towards the horse's mouth in a softening action but without dropping the contact.

Figure 2.6   The higher-held classical hand, centralized with the hands almost touching. When the horse moves in self-carriage this is the preferred hand position and brings lightness and elegance. To enhance self-carriage the rider lifts the hands up like a waiter offering a glass of champagne.

seat to the hands and so check that the horse is carrying his own head and neck. It is right when you can feel the bit resting in the horse's mouth through the rein.

The **torso** is placed centrally over the seat and can affect rider position dramatically. If you lean forwards it can put the horse on the forehand, if you sit too far backwards you ride behind the movement. The torso should lie on that imaginary vertical line that runs from the bottom up the back to the head. This is the line you use to maintain a correct position, only departing from it for specific reasons.

You can imagine you have a string attached to your tummy button and as the horse moves forwards this string is pulled, then released, thus the stomach goes forwards with the movement and returns to its original position. This imaginary string can be used by you especially in trot as an exercise to check you are sitting live with the horse. The movement of the horse moves through your seat, hips, tummy, and back, and when the movement is absorbed correctly it moves through so that you keep contact with the saddle at all times.

Keep your lower back upright so that the spine runs straight up from the seat. You may find it helpful to think of lifting the shoulders up and rolling them back and down, i.e. to stretch the shoulders wider. The shoulder blades will then come closer together. These suppling exercises help to keep your back upright and expand the chest up and forwards. If ever you doubt you are sitting upright think Mae West again! This is not a gimmick, these images create a picture you can relate to and make it easier to sit well when you are relaxed. To ride well you require good posture and good posture requires enough muscle tension to maintain your self-carriage in a coordinated and relaxed frame.

Another way to help you to sit straight and upright is to imagine that your ribcage is bigger than your chest. The diaphragm lifts. Hey presto, we have an upright classical riding position in a jiffy and it really is that simple.

The **legs** hang down naturally from the hips as if a rider were standing on the ground, but with a slight bend in the knees. If a rider's position is correct, if the horse were to shoot from under her seat she would land on her feet. If, however, the position is incorrect and the rider were sitting on her crutch she would land on her knees, and if sitting behind the vertical she would land on her bottom. This is a sobering thought! With the legs in the correct position and the knees positioned in the knee rolls, angles will be formed between the hip and the upper thighs, and the knees and the lower legs.

The rider's **thighs** lie flat against the saddle flap with the points of the knees facing forwards, and should not stick out leaving a gap between the rider's legs and the saddle. But neither should the thighs be pressed tightly against the saddle; they should cradle the horse in a way that allows the lower legs to remain relaxed and to lie against the sides of the horse.

Keeping the knees relaxed and nestled into the saddle flap positions the whole leg correctly, and they are only pointed outwards if the rider wants to tap the horse with the heels when, for example, asking a reluctant horse to canter. They are repositioned into the saddle flap immediately after this extra aid is given. The positioning and tension of the thighs also affects the seat. They should be held against the horse's sides in a soft and relaxed manner; if they grip the saddle too tightly they will push the rider's bottom out of the saddle, normally from the top of the thigh.

The **lower legs** hang down naturally with angles at the hip, knee and ankle. These angles depend on the width of the horse's barrel and the length of the rider's legs and also the depth of the seat being ridden. The line from the hip to the knee to the foot forms a V shape and the angle of the V will be shallow or pronounced depending on the factors named above. This angle anchors the rider's position and boosts the ability to sit with the horse's centre of gravity. The toes are positioned at a slight outward angle to the legs, but this must not be exaggerated to the point where the toes stick out in an ungainly manner – the toes-out position – and the legs come away from the sides of the horse. The opposite extreme is riding pigeon-toed with the toes sticking into the sides of the horse. It must be understood that unless the toes are positioned correctly the correct lower leg position is impossible, and minor adjustments like this can greatly improve riding.

The rider keeps the lower leg relaxed 'cuddling' the horse (Figure 2.7). When she wants to give leg aids the cuddle becomes firmer but should still be gentle and pleasant, making the horse feel, 'Ah, yes, I like that.' As soon as the leg aids have been applied by a firmer cuddle the muscle tension returns to the original soft cuddle.

To keep the lower legs soft the feet must be placed in the stirrup irons correctly, the base of the feet rest on the stirrups. The stirrups are used solely as foot rests and are not to be leant on with all the weight of the rider bearing down on them. The horse will feel this tension in his back more than if the rider is pushing vigorously with her seat, and riding in such a forceful manner stops the energy from coming through. If the feet rest lightly on the stirrups, when you place more weight into them it acts as a 'go' button asking the horse to move forwards, rather than applying the lower leg. This subtle aiding works well on sensitive horses who are hot and also with highly trained horses. For example, some stallions at the Spanish Riding School of Vienna move forward from the rider just placing more weight onto the stirrup through the big toes. However, a rider has to feel the sensitivity of a horse and understand that the normal forward-asking aids are the lower legs.

It is important that the ankles stay supple; they are a part of the body for which there are not many suppling exercises. It does, therefore, pay dividends

Figure 2.7   A relaxed soft leg with the lower leg on the girth and the toes positioned at a slightly outward angle. The normal relaxed soft leg position against the horse's sides is like giving him a cuddle.

The foot should not be positioned at too great an angle outwards because only the back of the calf muscles will come onto the saddle giving an inadequate leg contact. Also, if the toe is turned in, the calf muscles will come away from the saddle. If you grip the horse with your legs, it is the equivalent of making someone run a marathon while wearing a girdle.

The lower leg position depends on your height, length of leg, and the width of the horse. You will find some horses fit your leg perfectly but others have a round barrel so that wherever you position your leg, their sides seem to fall away from the leg. To counteract this, you may need a slightly shorter stirrup; for example, perhaps one to two holes shorter than that required with a narrow horse.

To measure the correct length of the stirrups before you mount, place your hand with the fingers tucked into the palm on the stirrup bar and the leather should be long enough to allow the stirrup tread to reach your armpit. When you mount, let your legs hang down loosely. The stirrup tread should be level with the part of your boot just above the sole but be flexible and if you feel you are reaching for your stirrups when the horse is moving, especially in trot and canter, shorten your stirrups so that they lie just below the ankle joint, or higher if necessary. It is better to have a secure safe seat and allow your leg muscles to stretch down gradually through practice than sit in a position that you consider classical but that your body cannot accommodate. In addition, the modern classical seat is an angled seat, i.e. not as straight-legged as formerly, and the amount of the angle in your leg joints depends on the horse and your shape, as already pointed out.

You will discover that the modern dressage saddle allows a longer leg and deeper seat, while keeping an angle between the thighs and the lower leg, although this angle might be only *slight* if you ride with your stirrup leathers at the longest length, your position will ensure it will still be there. The modern dressage saddle automatically helps anchor your dressage position. The saddle fitting the horse is more important than riding in a snazzy dressage saddle and sometimes you have to compromise. I have had students whose horses were happy in show-jumping saddles, and not so happy in dressage saddles, or the students could not afford to buy two saddles, and many of my students win loads of dressage rosettes with show-jumping saddles. I recommend that you buy a dressage saddle providing it fits you and your horse, and your pocket.

if a rider does ankle exercises when dismounted; this involves circling the ankles clockwise and anti-clockwise slowly five to ten times each, or massaging around the ankle joint. Keeping the ankles supple allows the energy to travel down the legs so that the ankles act like springs; as the movement comes down, the heel absorbs the movement. Stiff ankles stiffen the leg and deaden the sensitivity coming through to the stirrups from the seat. The heel should be lower than the toe, but some riders find it easier to think toe up rather than heel down. Also, the heel should not be pushed forcefully down or the leg will tense. If you have high arches, as many dancers do, a tip is to position the stirrup slightly more towards the toes than is classically correct, the rider will then find the weight is transferred to and absorbed by the heels more smoothly.

Application of the leg aids

Each horse is an individual and each has his sensitive spots. The rider's legs are positioned on the horse's sides in the natural way as described above and when the aids are to be applied she needs to be aware of the sensitive spots. Generally, these spots correspond to the accepted normal classical leg position, but some horses like the aids applied with the legs just a little forward of the normal shoulder–hip–heel-line leg position, (Figure 2.8), while other horses prefer the legs placed a little behind the normal position (Figures 2.9a and b). You will discover these sensitive spots by knowing your horse and from riding experience. Horses will assuredly let you know how things feel; for example, a ticklish mare will kick out at a leg applied too far back, or another horse may need a more positive touch to make him respond to the request to move forward (Figures 2.10a and b). The rider will have to experiment with these 'go' buttons (sensitive spots) in order to elicit the correct response. Generally horses are more sensitive around the girth area – hence the horseman's maxim, 'apply your leg on the girth.'

Some horses respond better to the on-off leg, which is a modern technique. The legs lie against the sides of the horse in the classical position but the leg is softer and more relaxed than with the cuddle, and the leg is put on and then taken off the horse's side.

When teaching the lateral aids or the outside canter aid, i.e. the aid given with the outside leg, the leg is positioned behind the girth (Figures 2.11a and b).

Figure 2.8 This photo taken at halt shows how *slightly* the leg should be positioned forward of the girth when riding round the corner looking for bend (i.e. asking for just a hint of bend) When you are riding to encourage bend, position your lower leg about ½–1 in (1–2.5 cm) in front of your normal leg position, closer to the front edge of the girth and as close to the first rib as you can manage. The first rib lies just in front of the girth. You can look for bend as you come into the apex of the corner by positioning your leg forward as described above and putting more weight into the inside seat bone. Remember to bring your shoulders and hips round to indicate to the horse the small amount of increased bend you want. For a few strides you are asking for more inside bend than normal, through the ribs, and through the front end of the horse; this is achieved by positioning a little more with the hands to the inside towards the horse's withers by ¼–½ in (approximately 1 cm). This is more a feeling than a movement because it is so tiny a movement so as not to disconnect from the outside contact. Or you can simply place more weight on the inside seat bone and/or inside stirrup by positively taking the hips and shoulders round a tiny amount to follow the increased bend through the horse's body and sitting more towards the new centre of gravity. When you ride this looking-for-bend movement, check that you straighten the horse as you come out of the corner to go large. You can combine this exercise with a slight positioning to the outside bend before you arrive at the corner, straight-

ening, and then looking for inside bend before the apex. It is best to do this exercise in walk initially, and to ensure you do not swing the horse's head from outside to inside bend, but do the movement slowly and precisely.

This looking for inside bend through the body is suppling the horse with minute movements of the body and typifies classical riding – less equals more, the simplicity of classical work. It helps straightness and softens the horse through the poll and to the mouth.

Figure 2.9a   This is the usual position when using the leg behind the girth, or for lateral-work aids. The less you position the leg behind the girth for the above aids, the more stable your position will remain, and the more effective your leg aids will be. Some horses will accept the leg 2–3 in (5–7.5 cm) behind the girth, others 4–6 in (10–15 cm). You have to find the spot that suits the horse. Mares often resent the lower leg being placed too far back, because it imitates the positioning of a stallion when he is mounting a mare, and they may swish the tail in annoyance. Be tactful and feel what suits your horse's body shape, attitudes, and understanding.

Figure 2.9b if the leg is positioned too far behind the girth it tips the rider to the outside and weakens the effectiveness of the lower-leg aids. But it can sometimes be used if a horse lacks understanding of lateral-work leg aids, or he has a long back. Always be sure it does not compromise your upper body position, and never use it for the outside-leg canter aid.

Figure 2.10a The inside leg is positioned in a close 'cuddle' around the horse's side to give a positive touch to ask him to come forward off the inside leg aid. For example, sometimes a horse resists the inside leg when you ask for canter, and a tap with the heel is all that is needed to get the horse moving forward. I emphasize that tap means *just a tap*, nothing more violent under any circumstances. Maybe the horse does not understand the aid or cannot feel it clearly. It is better to leave the spurs off for this aid and, if you do wear them, wear the nipple spurs, or rounded short spurs, and make sure you tap lightly and reposition the leg to the correct position immediately.

Figure 2.10b This photo shows the rider turning the toe out and heel in to give a correction tap with the heel to a horse who has been resistant to the inside leg aid of the canter aids.

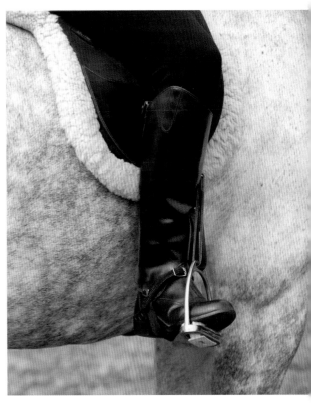

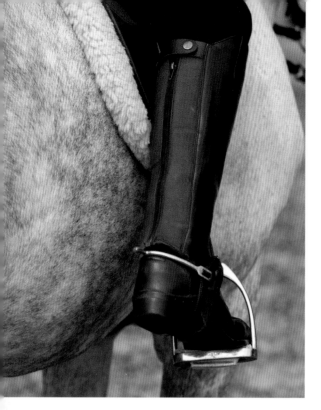

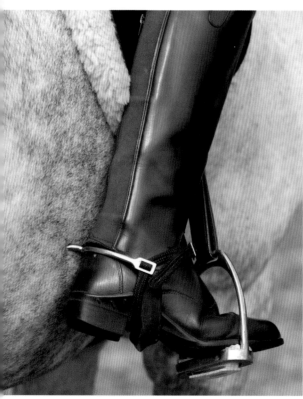

Figures 2.11 a and b   The outside leg is positioned behind the girth in preparation for teaching the sideways aids, e.g. leg-yields. Tuck the knee into the fold of the knee roll, lift the lower leg away from the horse's side, position it behind the girth and softly press (put the leg 'on') and release the leg with a gentle nudge, nudge action as you ask for the sideways steps. Avoid dragging the leg along the horse's side and gripping. Once the horse understands the aid with the leg applied 'on' behind the girth, you can position it further forward towards the girth and in a more positive and classical way, snugly feeling the horse's side.

This type of outside leg position is useful for developing the horse's reaction to the canter and, until the canter is straight, I prefer it to the normal canter aids with which some horses get confused and pick up canter on the wrong lead. Also, this modern barely applied outside leg aid teaches the horse the inside aids for canter more specifically and this is good because they are the dominant leg aids for canter. The benefit to the rider is that she avoids making a mistake with the aids by pushing the quarters over to the inside track, thus making the horse crooked. However, when you begin to teach the flying changes you need to teach both inside and outside leg aids in the normal way (i.e. the inside leg is positioned around the horse's side and the outside leg is applied in a light prepare-for-canter way). The reason it is preferable not to do it before is because to the horse the outside leg aid for canter feels very similar to the outside half-pass aid and this confusion should be avoided, otherwise he may come off the aids and do half-pass when you want flying changes and vice versa. If, however, you have already taught your horse the classical canter leg aids, stick to them but lighten the outside leg aid. You will discover it is easier to do it the lighter way.

It is important that a rider stays open to finding ways of riding to suit her horse, and adapts riding styles for the needs of different horses.

Confirming your Rider Position with Lungeing

Today people still enjoy lunge lessons because, as the control of the horse is in the trainer's hands, they can concentrate on establishing a secure riding position (Figure 2.12). The rider needs a reliable lunge horse for the lessons to be effective. Lunge lessons are especially good for children starting out with their riding because it gives them confidence (Figure 2.13). Lungeing can also help balance a pony who is too small to be ridden by an adult who may be too tall or heavy for him.

Figure 2.12 Confirm your position, especially whether or not you are sitting level, or faults such as collapsing your hips, shoulders tipping, and your weight carried to one side will happen.

LUNGEING GUIDELINES

1. The lunger must always wear gloves to avoid rope burn.
2. The horse should be lunged without the rider first to ensure the edge is taken off his freshness before the rider gets on.
3. A lunge whip is normally used, but discreetly. It is important that the lunger discovers prior to lungeing if the horse is familiar with the lunge whip, if he accepts it, or if he is frightened of it. If he is scared of it in any way it is better not to use it, but to use flicking motions with another lunge line, or flick with a schooling whip. When the lunge whip *is* used it should trail on the ground a short distance behind the hind legs of the horse. A friend of mine was famous for his lungeing techniques and people laughed to see cats playing with the end of his lunge whip as he walked into the dressage

Figure 2.13 Young Callum being warmed up on the lunge by mum ready for exercises.

arena. So take a tip from this expert and, before lungeing commences, remember to keep the lash of the whip trailing behind you and keep the whip tucked under your arm, pointing downwards so that the horse is not threatened by it. If you were to lift the point of the whip up and crack it, most horses would be terrified and it is important that the horse is happy to accept the cues from the whip. The lunge whip is used to indicate more forward movement and should only be used in a more insistent way with a horse who is blasé about the whip and even then *never* to frighten him. Only in extreme cases should a whip be cracked to ask a horse for more forward movement because there are so many other ways to ask for this.

4. Side reins should be used with the length adjusted so that the horse works in a round outline and should ensure that there is contact with a small amount of slack. To achieve this correct adjustment, put the side reins on, stand in front of the horse and take a side rein in each hand. Bring them towards your body by approximately 6 in (15 cm) so that they are not too

tight. This length is a guideline for when a horse is used to working in side reins. When he is learning to accept them, they should be fitted more loosely. Because the side reins encourage a horse to work better through his back, his back will be softer which, if you are being lunged, means that you can sit more easily in the saddle and communicate with the horse without causing counter-effects.

Unclip the side reins when the horse is working in walk so that you do not suppress the energy in the walk, but clip them on again when the horse is working in trot. Generally they are better unclipped for canter because the three-time movement of this gait can tend to encourage the horse to lean on the bit and puts him on the forehand, and obviously this is the opposite to what you want. Observe the reactions of your horse to being lunged with the side reins connected in canter and make a decision whether to have them clipped on or unclipped. Often it is simply a matter of what suits each horse and the handler should remain flexible to the needs of each horse. Trot is the best gait for lunge work with side reins because the two-time movement of this gait keeps the movement through the horse's body equal and more easily balanced than walk or canter. It also has the propensity to help contact and throughness. To observe safety regulations always unclip side reins before and while the rider is mounting and dismounting because if a horse spooks he will lift his head and may be frightened by the side reins tightening and the bit sticking in his mouth. In extreme cases this could result in him rearing up and even falling backwards.

5. For exercises when a rider is working without bridle reins, tie the ends of the reins in a knot. She holds the buckle end of the knotted bridle reins in her hand resting on the saddle. She is preparing for lunge exercises without the bridle reins but in an extreme case of a horse spooking she has the reins at hand to gather up and take control. This is a safety measure.

6. Start lunge exercises by walking the horse quietly so that the rider can get the feel of his strides in this slow gait while using the stirrups initially. Subsequently she slips her feet out of the stirrups and relaxes her leg down in a natural way.

7. Once the rider is relaxed and happy she is asked to retake the stirrups and

the horse is asked to move forwards into a brisk working trot. Again, the rider gets to feel the horse's movement without having to worry about control, and this gives her a sense of freedom in riding that she does not experience while riding normally.

8. The horse is now brought forwards to walk again and, providing the rider is happy, the reins are taken away by tying them in a knot (as explained above). The trainer can now start the pupil on arm and shoulder exercises in walk.

a) Stretching the arms up and round in circular movements (Figure 2.14).

b) Stretching the hand up and touching the toes.

c) Holding the arms up level with the shoulders and with the hands facing forwards. The rider then turns slowly from the waist keeping the arms held up, first to the inside, and then to the outside. This stretches the waist and shoulders, and helps balance.

Figure 2.14 Arm exercises on the lunge.

9. Exercises for the lower body can now begin, for example:

a) The rider brings the knees right up to the top of the saddle like a jockey, and then pushes the leg down towards the back of the saddle making sure the downward push does not come in front of the pommel. This exercise is best done in halt to begin with so that the lunger can show exactly what is needed. The rider does the exercise first with the inside leg and then with the outside one, but once she feels comfortable she can perform the exercise in walk, and with both legs together in halt first and then in walk. The advanced rider can perform this exercise in trot.

b) The rider points the toes down tensing the legs like pokers, and then gently shaking the tension free.

c) The above exercise can be followed by the rider imagining she has the legs of a rag doll, releasing all the tension and letting the leg muscles go floppy.

d) It is also good to do ankle exercises while riding: the rider takes them round in slow deliberate circles, first clockwise and then anti-clockwise.

Combining leg-tensing exercises with soft absolutely-no-tension exercises contracts and softens the leg muscles, so that when the rider retakes her stirrups she should be able to relax the legs down and around the horse in a better way: the outline of her legs against the horse should appear crisp and more defined, yet the leg action is softer and more effective.

10. The teacher finishes the lunge lesson by asking the rider to ride holding the reins and using the stirrups as if she were riding off the lunge. She rides forwards into walk and trot and should now feel the benefit of the exercises and how they have affected her riding position.

11. The side reins are unclipped before the rider is allowed to dismount for the safety reasons mentioned in point 4.

The trainer must not overdo the length of the lunge lesson. Normally, the first lesson would be fifteen minutes and progress to a maximum of thirty minutes for an established rider. Lungeing is not only more demanding for the horse, but also requires more concentration from the rider who will often be using muscles in a way she has not before, and to avoid muscle cramp she should take it steady. If the rider does get cramp (and this can happen particularly in the hips because with dressage the hips are used in a coordinated way that is not echoed in many other exercises) then the teacher must bring the horse to halt and allow the rider to stretch her legs. Normally, the cramp will disappear immediately, but if it does not it is better for the rider to dismount, and do exercises on the ground to stretch her legs, especially the upper thighs and hips. The lunge lesson should be left for another day.

Riding in Harmony

A rider sits in harmony with the horse. Avoid propping yourself in the saddle by hanging on to the reins or gripping with the legs. Sitting in harmony with the horse gives him the freedom to move in an expressive way (Figure 2.15). A good dressage position comes from balance not gripping, from posture not tension.

It is perhaps advisable for a rider to begin a dressage career riding just one horse until she is familiar with his movements, and the different aspects of dressage riding, but once she starts to progress, riding different types of horses will help her improve. When a rider has reached a competent level she may find it useful to ride only a few horses during a particular period because the one-to-one relationship between horse and rider is special, and that special closeness should not be inhibited. This closeness is magnified in dressage, and the rider should aim to deepen this relationship.

Having said that riding different horses improves your riding once you have reached a decent level of competence, sometimes the reverse is true. Once you have advanced say to Grand Prix level you might want to limit the amount of horses you ride. For example, Margit Otto-Crepin rode only her Grand Prix horse, Corlandus, because he was so talented it was like driving a Ferrari, she could only ride him, and riding other horses would have jeopardized this relationship. Riders should decide what horses they ride, and how many, and not be pressured by others into riding horses that do not suit them. The classical schools subscribe to this way of thinking, selecting the right horse for a rider, because they know the wrong horse can affect riding ability.

Figure 2.15 Horse and rider in harmony. The rider sits a little forward to help this young horse who finds it difficult to round in canter.

Horses and riders must suit each other in temperament and physique and, although good training teaches a rider to control her temperament (and this widens the field for selecting the right horse), there is still an indefinable quality that must be taken into account. You can look at a horse and be instantly aware that you like a horse; you want to ride that horse, and feel that that horse will take care of you. This sensitivity is an important part of riding and should not be overlooked. Stay open to what your senses are telling you, stay open to what the horse is telling you, use your common sense, and make an informed decision about what horses you want to ride.

A rider must be honest about her stage of riding, and look for ways to lift herself to the next level but without putting herself under too much stress. She wants the challenge without the strain, progression not regression, and wants to grow in confidence and knowledge so that her skills improve.

MUTUAL UNDERSTANDING

Young horses benefit from experienced riders, but they can be tempted to push the youngsters too quickly in their training; consequently a less experienced rider can often do a better job under the guidance of an experienced rider. On the contrary, an advanced horse needs an advanced rider because a novice can undo a good horse's training in seconds by applying the wrong aids. A good schoolmaster, however, can make a rider. Ideally, a horse's training should be a few stages higher than the rider's level, but this is not always possible.

As you can see, there are many situations to consider. It can be that a rider likes a horse even if he seems unsuitable, because their attitudes suit each other and the pair get on and progress well. Minds must remain open to possibilities, and this open-mindedness is an integral part of dressage.

RIDER 'FEEL'

'Feel' is a nebulous, cloudy entity, and it can be difficult to explain. Feel is critical to good dressage yet my perception of feel may differ from yours. How do we teach people to recognize feel? It seems beyond explanation and is peculiar to each rider.

Dressage is a tactile art; to develop feel we need to practise in a way that produces good quality work, and to do this we utilize riding situations that will let us experience feel. For example, I ask a student to ride a transition and then ask them how it felt, but at the same time I indicate the results she got. Once she has progressed I will ask her to give herself dressage marks for movements, and to quantify why she has done so. This develops her ability to equate the feel of a movement with comments, and with causes and effects, and to know that an informed eye is watching her from the ground. This is one of the reasons why dressage riding progresses more easily with a trainer. It is possible to be self-taught – there have been good self-taught riders who have ridden Advanced dressage – although it is more difficult, and it is less fun to achieve this than when working as a team of horse, rider, and trainer.

Aids are the language we use to communicate our riding instructions to the horse. By applying them we get responses from the horse, and we feel these responses. The horse learns by the correct application of the aids, i.e. the correct repetition of aids for each exercise. We should acknowledge that the horse will feel different some days; for example, he may feel lively one day and tired the next, but generally he will feel the same, especially if he has been well trained.

Dressage is technique, experience, and feel. Every situation and response will give us a different feel and we need to build a library of sensations. This takes time plus the experience of riding different horses in different dressage exercises. The more we learn the more we realize that small adjustments in our riding can make huge differences. Less equals more in dressage, and when we have felt it we can pat ourselves on the back. It is a wonderful feeling to place a tiny bit more weight on the stirrup and your horse moves actively forwards, it is great to lift your hands just a quarter of an inch to encourage self-carriage and feel the horse lighten and come into beautiful balance. Feel comes from experience, but it is essential to have the *right* experiences, which explains why some riders never progress. Training sifts out the bad and keeps the good, because good repetition gives quality feel.

General Information

FITNESS

Dressage demands its own fitness. It is not the fitness of the marathon runner or the weight lifter, for example, but it requires some respiratory fitness, suppleness, a sense of balance (like skiers), good coordination (like dancers), and good body posture (like gymnasts). Dressage is good exercise for old and young alike and all can compete; for example, many children under ten compete, there have been Olympic riders of over 72 years of age, and many riders who began Advanced dressage at 65 were, within a few years, competing at Grand Prix level. All these statistics prove that dressage is a sport for everyone; it is growing every year but is not yet wholly discovered and tried.

SAFETY AND COMFORT

A good riding position is better than any crash helmet, and we must always think of safety when riding a horse. Do you know that riding is nearly as dangerous as motor racing? The horse travels at speed and forces of gravity sometimes insist we fall off – and this can hurt, besides being dangerous – but if we develop a good dressage seat the chances of falling are reduced dramatically. If you focus on learning dressage just to get an independent seat you will be helping yourself.

Be comfortable when you are riding, feel like you are wearing comfortable shoes, the type you would take a long walk in or sit and watch television in. Comfort is critical to good riding and good training. A rider must feel comfortable riding a horse and the horse must feel comfortable being ridden; dressage is not about causing discomfort or pain, it is like dancing, an expression of joy. There will be days when you push yourself harder, but if you push too hard, not only will *you* get torn muscles, cramp and feel stressed, but you may also cause your horse strains and upsets. Build up fitness gradually and then you will tone up the right muscles rather than damaging them. It takes time for riding muscles to tone up and it is better to build up the tone gradually than slog away and get aches and pains. Strained muscles fray self confidence. Nobody acquires a good riding position overnight but with steady practice the rider becomes competent, and this competence improves through experience. Progress in a positive way that is practical to your situation and you will progress quicker.

3 WORKING IN HARMONY

BE FREE IN your inner to be a winner,' a great dressage rider said. Enjoy your training and be in harmony with your horse. Experience a freedom that allows talents a free rein, no exercise is too difficult, no horse limited, no situation too daunting – this freedom releases the rider to absorb the truth. Dressage becomes fun (Figure 3.1).

Positive Learning

Be positive; always ride with a big smile on your face. A smiley image is an essential symbol for the discerning dressage rider (Figure 3.2); she can have all the brains, brawn, and ability in the world, but if she lacks positivity she is standing on the quay watching the boat sail away. She can wait, of course, for another boat to arrive – there are never negatives in dressage!

How do we work in harmony? Deep down in our hearts we have to understand the strengths and weaknesses of our horses and of ourselves, sink deep into the ethos of training, and develop focus and meditation. This ability to concentrate is integral to good dressage riding, and nothing of value can be achieved without it. But we need to practise to get it; it takes work to acquire this asset. It is like producing an oil painting: First you draw the sketch and then you apply layer upon layer of fine oil paint, which allows the gloss to shine through. Not only are we training the physiques of horse and rider whenever

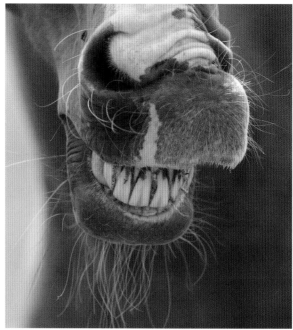

Figure 3.1 (Left)   Having fun with a pas de deux.

Figure 3.2 (Above)   Straight from the horse's mouth: just laugh when things go wrong, and carry on with your training; learning should be fun!

we ride, but we are strengthening character, building relationships, and widening our horizons. Dressage is multi-faceted, the best sport can offer.

THE TRAINING ETHOS

The willingness to learn is the key to success. Dressage means to train, yet training is a two-way process: to learn through instruction and to instruct. First we resemble pieces of blotting paper absorbing and sucking up instruction, but once the blotting paper is saturated we are ready to open ourselves to deeper forms of training, such as teaching, which is a great way to continue learning. We never stop learning in dressage, but we must learn to walk before we run. A lack of submission will stifle our learning ability; we need, therefore, to be respectful of established knowledge and this takes three forms..

1. To respect others and ourselves, not condemning our abilities, but encouraging the process of learning (Figure 3.3).
2. To respect our horses, to understand that they are learning too, and to offer them opportunities to improve in a natural, progressive way.
3. To respect our teachers by not just taking out the bits of their training that we want, but by embracing the whole package, and sticking to one trainer for a reasonable length of time so that this process can take place. (Trainer hopping is not conducive to good learning, but then neither is being trained by the wrong trainer, and so this needs to be gauged carefully.)

A lack of respect will block learning. If we face weaknesses, and build on strengths, progress will be obvious. Dressage is like skiing; if we have the confidence to ski down the steepest slopes, advancement comes. The understanding trainer knows when to push the rider, and when to spoon feed her. It is good to listen and learn and also to ask questions but do not use

Figure 3.3 Mother and son together, learning from each other.

them as excuses, because if you are constantly asking 'why' instead of trusting the trainer and getting on with the job in hand, then the path to learning will not lie straight before you. Ask a few questions if you don't understand the specific exercise you are being taught, do the practical application and then you will discover that the exercises themselves supply the answers. All other questions should be asked after the lesson, or thought through between training sessions. This shows intelligence and a desire to learn, and will encourage your trainer to think through your particular riding problems on your behalf. Trainers are human beings too, and also need encouragement; they make mistakes, have bad hair days, and excel at other times. When you do have questions, think of you, the horse and the trainer as one unit, and solve the problems as a team.

There are many techniques, many riding sessions to go through, before we gel with our horses and break through to that wonderful feeling of divine sensation I have talked about, but a lack of respect will dismantle it. We want to go forwards in big strides (like the horse!) to cover the ground beautifully. Save the adrenaline rush for special occasions, and keep riding sessions for learning and enjoyment. Keep minds, muscles, and sinews, relaxed. Work at a rate that suits your particular needs, a crucial part of healthy dressage development. Dressage cannot be forced, yet sometimes we observe the opposite, because today we demand speed – our culture is focused on making things happen quickly. We throw a ready-meal in the microwave, we switch on mobiles, we fly to the other side of the world – all in a flash – we are programmed into thinking fast is best, but the human physiology has not advanced to keep step with speed (nor has that of the horse) and if we are not careful we achieve nothing by going faster. At the same time if we are nervous about trying new exercises we will never progress. 'Resting is rusting,' is a good maxim, to advance the right way.

Do not underestimate the importance of absorbing the ethos of training, or you will flounder and hit frustrations, but if you embrace it the training brings tremendous fun and rewards. All sports incorporate areas of learning, but dressage is wholly concerned with it; competition is simply the cherry on the cake. Although you should reach a decent level of competence before competing, competition motivates and, if approached in a positive way, teaches quality.

THE LEARNING CIRCLE

This circle is divided into quarters; each quarter representing a stage of learning:

Stage 1 We start riding at the **unconsciously incompetent** quarter.

Stage 2 As we learn we realize we have inadequacies and we know we can correct them. At this point we are **consciously incompetent** riders. This quarter covers a long period of training, the blotting-paper stage, and we should not be discouraged, but soak up instruction and enjoy it.

Stage 3 Once we start to become dressage riders and can 'feel' and are able to ride and identify causes and effects of the mistakes being made, then we become **subconsciously competent** riders. The majority of good riders stay at this stage. They may compete at Novice or Grand Prix level, but are competent without knowing precisely why. They do everything automatically without thinking about it. They can ride a half-pass while blowing their noses, or do a walk-to-canter transition while discussing politics with a friend. Correct coordination is imbedded in the subconscious mind; it appears like an innate instinct, as though the rider was born on the horse. There is no thinking, no struggle, everything is easy.

The leap from **consciously incompetent** to **subconsciously competent** can take anything from three to thirty years of riding. You can feel pleased about reaching this stage and give yourself a pat on the back. You may not be riding piaffe, but you are a good rider. Be encouraged, we can all reach Stage 3 with patience and application. Nobody can take it away from you.

But if you are already riding at the third stage let me encourage you to take the final step to Stage 4. It opens up many exciting possibilities and does not apply solely to the cream of the dressage world but to you also; be positive, reach out for it!

Stage 4 The last stage is being **consciously competent**, and is the ultimate stage for the dressage rider, when every subconscious action should be boiled down and questioned in order to improve it. A rider may want to teach at this point because it helps the process of making the leap from the third to the fourth stage, or to write about the subject because you have to analyze every nuance of dressage riding. This is the stage when the rider can go from skilled rider to artist.

Whichever stage you attain, nobody can steal your competence. It is like riding a bicycle – once you have done it you can always do it. If you have a break, get fit and start again. Dressage is done by different types of people, from different backgrounds, and of different ages. There is no limit; as your confidence grows, you may reach for a new challenge, which will push you to a different level of learning. We work through the circle of learning within the confines of our abilities.

Learning rates

We travel from each learning stage to the next at different rates. Sometimes we accelerate up the curve within each stage quickly and that can give a buzz – a 'yippee' feeling that makes learning fun. But sometimes we reach a plateau and feel that we cannot break away from the staleness of the place where, we think, we are stuck, but this is a fallacy. All that might be needed is a prod to get us going up the curve again, even though we may need to keep plodding along the plateau for a while initially, and that is okay too. A sympathetic trainer will identify whether you need a push to get you going on the upward curve again, or whether you need to consolidate and just keep travelling along that plateau line for a while.

Bringing in new ways to enjoy dressage can help if you feel you have reached a stalemate. Sometimes we need to kick-start our learning, to crank it up like an old 1950s car. We can all reach a stalemate but it should not cause despair. Find a sympathetic friend, or trainer, and have a long talk about the problem; sit down and think carefully, and experiment a little to work out your next move.

Watching others ride may help, as may reading books and articles by, and about, other riders to glean tips. You might just need to add some more notches to your competition-dressage belt or to ride advanced horses, or try a new trainer, or have lessons more frequently. The answer may take time to evolve but be encouraged, everybody learns and progresses within the learning circle at their own particular rate, and we all move up the learning curves at our own speed too. Some learn quickly, some more slowly, some learn particular movements quickly and other movements slowly, but you cannot judge learning by speed, only by the quality. This is another beauty of dressage.

Dressage is **training – training, training,** and training is **balance – balance, balance.** This equation between training and balance helps cement the relationship between the horse and rider. Dressage is not about winning, it is about 'holding hands' with the horse. Never be too ambitious too quickly. This leads to rules and regulations being adapted to protect horses from the minority of riders who make life intolerable for their horses because of misguided ambition, and it often makes animal lovers sigh with exasperation. So, to avoid being too demanding, adjust your ambitions to match abilities. For example, if your horse does well at dressage but is obviously not a potential Advanced competition horse, do not get angry with him and/or push him beyond his capabilities. A way to avoid such pitfalls is to have friends who can be your eyes on the ground. Such friendship keeps you steadfast.

Training requires trust: the student trusting the trainer to step in if things go wrong, trusting friends to point out if things go wrong, and trusting her own instincts when all around her persist in saying the opposite. Gradually, learning to trust will come from experience and confidence. Many good riders reach a particular level and their training reaches a block because there has been lack of trust; they just need a helping hand to be more trusting. Make 'em laugh, make 'em cry, expel the poisons from the system, and you free the blockage. Sometimes something as simple as a helping hand is all that is needed. Self-sufficiency is dangerous because dressage is not about self-sufficiency but the companionship of horse and rider joining forces in order to travel to deeper understanding.

When we apply this constructive attitude we embark on a journey of learning of skills and character, and riding opens our minds to concentration, stillness, peace and enjoyment, which will spill out into other areas of our lives.

MAKE HASTE SLOWLY

Make haste slowly is a German proverb, meaning take things one step at a time. The slowest route is better and it gets you to your destination quicker. Each step is followed by the next consecutive step, and so on; each learning step is linked to the next one. The rider should visualize the end picture but plan the route towards it slowly. Training for dressage is like putting a jigsaw puzzle together; you look at the picture on the front of the box, you put the four corner pieces into place, and by then putting each piece of the jigsaw into its right place the picture gradually builds up and can be finished. If, however, you try to force pieces into the wrong places the jigsaw cannot be completed.

You may feel sorry for the rider who rushes things, because you know she will hit a point when she will have to start again to get it right, whereas if she had started correctly in the first place this would have been unnecessary. Once you have to start again, it often takes twice as long to make progress.

Dressage is healthy beautiful movement and riders who want the best for their horses are happy to make haste slowly. They do not renege on their responsibility to teach the horse. They are not weak-livered riders who back away from following the right way. Sometimes they even have to tell their friends politely, 'No, I'm not rushing my horse; I'm going to miss that show this season, perhaps we can compete later in the year.' Their friends may even think they are being silly, but once the end results are seen, the mocking smiles are wiped off their faces. The horse's performance speaks volumes; he will show how dedicated the rider has been.

A healthy relationship between horse and rider promotes understanding and mutual respect. Both have a sense of dignity, and both want to guard this dignity against outside forces that can so easily unravel years of hard work. Sometimes it is difficult to say no, but sometimes that is the best way forwards. Say yes to quality training, patience and perseverance, and then you will discover you are on track for competing successfully. It is worth the wait.

The horse does not understand that we live in the twenty-first century, we cook food in a microwave, and we have flown to the moon. He lives in a natural world where life is the same as it was yesterday, the day before, the decades before, and the centuries before that. He is centred on now, on being natural, on movement, on eating grass, on breathing fresh air, and he accommodates our strange behaviour because he is so tolerant. Every horse has a big generous heart that you only usually find in the likes of Saint Theresa of India. We owe him loyalty, consideration and understanding; if we stop rushing, we can develop these qualities far quicker.

Timescales

Today we are driven by timescales. Perhaps it would help to have an idea of the time it should take to train a horse, yet there is no defined answer.

When I was young and watching my mother cooking, I would ask, 'How long before it's ready?'

'When it's ready' came the answer. This would irritate me.

'An hour, two hours? Give us a clue!'

But she stubbornly insisted, 'When it's ready.'

I now understand exactly what she meant because her answer applies to dressage training, but I have given approximate guidelines to give you some idea of timescales so that you can develop a more sensitive feel for the time needed. These guidelines are based on the standard dressage competition levels.

Normally, it takes six months to a year to back a young horse and get him going well in his basic training; add another year to reach competent Novice level, and then add a year for each level of training after that. This rule applies for general training and competition levels. However, if a horse is talented he will advance more quickly, but beware of rushing the basic stages.

Another consideration is that talent cannot be measured by the time it takes to learn, although often the more talented horses do seem to progress quicker. This rule also applies to riders; some learn well but slowly, and some scoot through quickly. I never judge a horse or rider by their rate of learning, but by the quality of the work.

For example, my mare, Kashmir, took two years to learn the basics, but she learnt them so well she was brilliantly balanced even at Novice standard – light and obedient in self-carriage. She gave a wonderful feeling of power.

NOTE TAKING

Few people are endowed with excellent memory and note taking allows the rider to relive riding situations, and to think through new ones. Notebooks become living diaries, memories recalled, and can give great joy to learning dressage.

You have heard of the expression, 'not being able to see the wood for the trees' and this can happen unless you have checks with which to avoid this situation; note taking is one of these checks. For example, if we hit a problem with collected canter we can return to working canter and trot-to-canter and walk-to-canter transitions to overcome problems in the canter. This gives direction, and often it gives us additional ways to make improvements.

My notebooks are a helpful source for future trouble-shooting. The following examples are notes on training.

- Sit back more in all canter work.
- Transitions to practise gaining fluidity, e.g. trot to canter. Collected canter work afterwards and canter pirouettes.
- More transitions to halt, and from trot to half-halts to encourage activity and balance.
- Walk out on the roads on a long rein for 10 minutes and then in contact on the bridle for 5 minutes. Then ride the trot very forwards and on up to the bridle
- Walk is improved by riding on a long rein. **Remember to start all sessions on a long rein and to end on a long rein**.
- A very marked improvement in trot and trot-to-canter transitions.

Tailor a notebook to your particular needs, write comprehensive or shortened notes, whichever you prefer, and make it a fun exercise. When a notebook is full, type up the notes and create a horse file for each horse. You can add observations as you progress, and keep it to reflect on. Include future directions and aims and suggested timescales for reaching them, plus other relevant tips. Avoid being too rigid with the notes, use them as a springboard to new thoughts and ideas.

Classical riders say, 'There is no dressage without practice, but there is no practice without theory.' You will lack an understanding of cause and effect if you do not understand theory, and find yourself going down blind alleys of training. Franz Rochowansky, a former Chief Rider at the Spanish Riding School of Vienna, told me that a large slice of his apprenticeship meant passing theory exams at high percentage passes. (If an apprentice did not achieve a high pass mark he was rejected and could not go on with his Spanish Riding School training.) He was encouraged to use notebooks and he continued adding to the notes for many years after he left the school. He used them to refer to if a riding problem arose and to keep his thinking attuned to good training.

So, let me encourage you to go and buy that notebook and make quick notes after each training session. Keep it in the tack box or tack room because then you will never forget to top up your notes after each session.

THE LINE OF AUTHORITY

Dressage has always been taught by trainer to student. Today, we have access to modern training props such as clinics, demonstrations, books, and videos, and they are helpful, yet they never replace the closeness of trainer and student. A training triangle of communication between the forces of horse, rider, and trainer develops, i.e. teamwork.

Training requires this line of authority: trainer, rider, and horse but if this line of authority is upset, the training will suffer (Figure 3.4). It is not oppression but authority that gives respect. Authority is not an excuse for over-zealous

Figure 3.4   Pep talks with the trainer during lessons consolidate the understanding of the work and give you and the horse a breather.

training, but overcoming riding problems with a sensible approach. Quick eloquence guides the team through pitfalls, but if the rider starts dictating to the trainer what should happen, the authority line is broken, and the training will go astray. So choose a trainer you respect, and respect this line of authority. You will become friends, but there has to be order.

I like a cooperative easy relationship with students and I like to see them laughing and enjoying their riding. I know I am winning when they start to suggest ways of doing things that are just right for the situation, and I will encourage them to think/ride through situations when we discuss matters. Overall, I have discovered the trainer has to be strong but in a firm kind way. It is not about being overtly strict but about controlling emotions so that a rider can work within the disciplined confines of dressage. There are many riders, particularly young riders, who have not experienced discipline in their lives and they often struggle with training when they first begin. Discipline is essential to dressage, and such riders may need to focus on becoming disciplined before they progress, but once their work improves, they thank me for teaching them this aspect of dressage training that is so essential.

I have been quite amused by the escalating number of television programmes dedicated to parents experiencing problems with bringing up their children. They call on a professional nanny, for example, who steps in and curbs the problem children, and shows the parents how to adjust their approaches to discipline. Yet I wonder if this process is possible over short periods of time? Surely, only continuous steady relationships are the answer otherwise the reactions to sudden changes are too violent. It is well to be flexible within the line of authority: never underestimate the power of being polite, for example. Manners maketh the man, and dressage helps foster good character.

Be consistent; consistency wins through. You must have time to learn – do not rush the process – and continue to take lessons. Don't set unrealistic aims, but make your ambitions bite-sized so that you can realize them. If you incorporate this programme into your training you will be surprised at the rate you progress.

The training environment of rider, horse, and trainer must be maintained but there are more dimensions to training than just riding; friends and family can also be part of the team (Figures 3.5a–e).

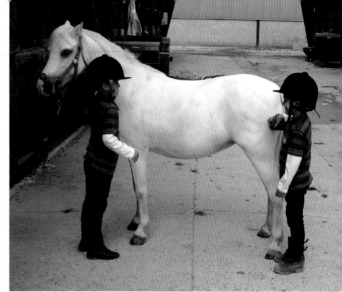

Figure 3.5a–e   Friends and family are part of the team and everyone should work as a team: Tina helping me on a photo-shoot day, twins Connor and Charlie groom together, mother and daughter and mother and son enjoy a mutual interest, and partners work together to help the rider of the pair perform better dressage; one rides and the other grooms.

SELECTING A TRAINER

You may like to consider the following points before selecting a trainer.

- Get a trainer that suits your needs now and for a few years ahead.
- You must feel comfortable with your chosen trainer so that you can discuss problems with them.
- Training is personal, and unless you connect with one another the communication will be fuzzy.
- Be practical. Take into account, for example, how far do you have to travel for each lesson? Will the trainer come to your yard? How much is each lesson? The actual amount is only relative to the value you receive, and the cheapest is not necessarily the best, but neither necessarily is the most expensive. You need to be able to afford regular lessons but remember that one quality lesson is worth handfuls of mediocre ones.
- Your horse should like the trainer too.
- Consider the background of the trainer and her methods. For example, be wary of an instructor who claims to have reinvented the wheel, because it is not possible in dressage, and, therefore, not honest. All dressage is based on classical principles, and the differences lie in the emphasis a trainer may put on certain aspects of training, or the leaning towards competition or classical training. All good trainers teach the same principles. There is no room for deviates in dressage.
- Go and watch the trainer work, or ask a student's opinion.

Get the best trainer you can afford, and stick to that person for at least two years. The better your riding becomes the higher the level of trainer you need; she should be at least two stages higher than the level at which you are working. For example, she should be at least established at Novice level to teach you Preliminary-level riding.

You will find plenty of good trainers available. Speak to them and explain what you want, and ask if they would be interested in training you. If you have a trainer already, mention that fact; it is polite to do this and quality dressage trainers will always appreciate it. Be considerate to everybody; a relationship is two sided – both parties need to feel happy.

The challenge is getting the training you need, and not some supposed idea of training you have dreamt up from watching top riders doing Grand Prix freestyle to music, for example, but a workable way of training as a team that makes it fun to learn. Think about your and your horse's needs and then see if the trainer you have selected fits the bill. Can she give you what you want? Is she the best quality you can afford? As I said, stick with the same trainer until you find that perhaps they cannot take you on to the next challenge, but if you do change trainers be sure you are not changing because you cannot confront your weaknesses.

Investing money in your training is never wasted. The best safety 'kit' you can have is a good riding position – it will outdo a good riding hat any day. I think it is a sad thing that people throw money at things like expensive rugs and jodhpurs, yet scrimp on paying for lessons. Dressage is about learning to ride well; why not focus a sensible expenditure on getting some good training? It makes sense.

SELECTING A STUDENT

I have talked about the aspect of the student looking for a trainer, but what about the trainer's viewpoint.

- I like a student who is loyal and I like her to be consistent. This does not mean that she has to spend oodles of money on lessons, but that she has a specific aim, a programme worked out, and that she does her best to stick to this programme, showing a professional attitude to her training.
- I love novice riders, but I like them to be keen. I want a student to practise the exercises we have gone through, but I understand that sometimes modern life makes it difficult and I am not, therefore, inflexible. But I do like her to have reasonable facilities in which to work because without them good dressage is difficult.
- I like her to arrive with clean tack that fits the horse correctly, and with clean riding gear, which should comprise riding gloves, a riding hat, jodhpurs, and either half chaps and jodhpur boots, or boots. I do not mind if she

does not carry a whip or wear spurs, but if a whip is carried, I prefer a short whip to be used with a young horse.

- I like her to be punctual, and to know how to warm up correctly, although I like her to walk her horse on a long rein before I start the lesson.
- I am very happy if a student asks questions, no matter how silly she may consider them; it shows intelligence and that she is thinking about her riding.
- I encourage a student to accept that she will make mistakes and to think them through. I like her to laugh, I do not even mind if she takes the mickey out of me to get her laughing.
- I like a rider to be kind to a horse and draw the line at overuse of the whip, or cruel use of the spurs.
- Riders should be effective, and I hate riders who swan about giving the impression that dressage is nothing more than looking pretty.
- I like politeness, but I do not mind if I am shouted at by a rider who is angry or frustrated (I prefer this sort of honesty to lukewarm insincerity).
- I want people to be passionate about dressage, to enjoy it, and to have fun.
- I am open to new ideas and approaches if they can be quantified in a logical way.
- I like riders who consider me part of the team and who ask me for advice outside the lesson.
- I understand learning is different for everyone and will accommodate a rider's individual needs; there is no point in trying to fit a round peg in a square hole.
- I prefer my students to use a kind bit, because I hate anything that causes pain to a horse. Occasionally, a horse benefits from being ridden in a gadget, but I like students to ask permission to use a particular gadget before they arrive for a lesson with it fitted on their horse.
- I am not happy to teach students who ride roughshod over their horses and their trainers – and I am inclined to let them know this. I am presenting a particular picture of how to train, and it is important that the student understands, accepts and immerses herself in this way of thinking so that when she is training on her own, I know the ideas and methods are carried on.

- I have rarely had to deal with aggressive riders because, thankfully, they are few and far between. A trainer puts her heart into teaching; she should feel that she is respected, as she respects her student. Training should be a healthy two-way relationship that benefits both persons.

EXPERIMENTING

You are free to experiment with ways of riding once you have reached a good level of competence. Indeed, it is healthy to do so, and a classical idea that should be encouraged. Make sure you base new ideas around proven ones, otherwise the training will unravel; think about the difficulty of picking up lost stitches when knitting. If we want to grow we should be brave enough to experiment. It is part of dressage training. Bounce ideas off your trainer, and see where they take you but be prepared to stop anything *immediately* if it is not working. You have sound basics to work from and nothing harmful will happen if you remain open to following the classical approach and blending it with the modern.

Students usually start to experiment after a year of training, and I encourage it. They might introduce new aspects of training in between lessons, and then check the work with me during a lesson. I am glad to listen to their viewpoints and look at the work, and unless something goes against basic dressage principles I never object; but I will say if they have gone completely wrong, explain why it was wrong and put it right. This process is beneficial to learning, it embeds the basics, and it brings riders back to the truths of dressage, which should be firmly secured in the student's psyche now.

Dressage is not tight boundaries or square boxes, but freedom and expression. The basic classical principles are cleaned up in training, and experimentation is growth, not crazy ideas or going off at a tangent. When the student feels free to reach out to experiment it shows trust between student and trainer, but the trainer should never adopt the arrogant attitude of 'I'm the trainer and I'm right, you are the student and you are wrong.' It is so tempting for a trainer to open their mouth and correct a student but, no matter how off-beat an idea may be, the trainer must listen to what the student has to say; she might surprise her trainer and teach her something new. Dressage is freshness and newness in motion. It takes moral integrity to go there.

FOCUS AND MEDITATION

Dressage can lead you towards meditation, if you allow it. Learning to concentrate is part of dressage, an important part, and meditating when you ride is important. Immersing yourself in the exercise you are involved in, excluding other thoughts and stimuli and yet being aware of everything that is happening around you is the only way you can keep on top of potential upsetting situations. This ability requires a fine degree of concentration but it does come with practice, you do not have to be registered with Mensa to do it. Do remember that the moment you put your feet in the stirrups you must allow dressage to wash over you; get rid of all thoughts of 'what ifs', the day's work/activities, arguments with partners or spouses and all other intrusive thoughts. Relax, take a deep breath and enjoy the moments of riding your horse.

Some people have a natural ability to concentrate but *all* dressage riders need to develop this skill. Horses also need to deepen their concentration, and this is not easy with a flight-from-danger animal. Here are some tips.

- Keep focused on what is happening underneath your seat, on how the horse is moving, and if he is going the way he should.
- Stay alert to what is happening around you in the immediate vicinity as well as keeping an eye on the horizon, because horses' eyes can take in a viewing field of nearly 360 degrees and they constantly scan the horizon to watch for predators. Only then can you can keep the horse alert and focused on your instructions and calm and attuned to them. If you are two steps ahead of him you can pre-empt anything he might spook at and either move away from it, ride him on the aids more, half-halt, or perform transitions or another exercise, but keep him alert to your riding aids, not his surroundings. Gradually, even the scattiest horse will become more focused.
- Combine the above concentration with being focused on your trainer. It is like having an invisible string connecting you, the horse, and the trainer. It takes practice, but with time you will reap the rewards. It is an exciting feeling being connected to this invisible string of communication, and another joy of dressage training.

Do not worry if you struggle to concentrate (some of the very best riders started with the concentration of a gnat) being scatterbrained is not a fault but being unwilling to correct it is a fault and so do not restrict your progress because you back away from concentration.

We live in a stressful fast environment today – lifestyles chip away at our peace of mind, and calmness is viewed as belonging to people of past years – but if you can just learn to concentrate, and allow the meditation to overtake your worries you will find dressage is calmness and beauty. Just try it and see.

I had to learn how to do this too; I live in a frantic, busy world of dog-eat-dog just the same as you do but the moment I ride I am enveloped in calmness, and this ability has spilled out into other areas of my life: writing, painting, and

Figure 3.6   Huggy Bear!

thinking. Be in control of your emotions but do not exclude them, be aware of your mindset but do not let it overtake you. These are all assets that develop better dressage riding.

Being hyper means you react to the stimulus around you in an automatic way; it is better if you are proactive because it allows you to be considerate of your needs and those of the horse. But being reactive obscures these needs, it tends to squeeze you into a shape you are not and this lacks compassion for yourself and the horse. So avoid riding with a rush-rush attitude, a pushy-pushy mindset, and step away from the stress. The French School, for example, taught riders to stay calm, but if they got stressed they were advised to smoke a cigarette. This is not something that is likely to be advised today but the idea is clear; the moment you feel tense, chill out! Tell a joke, do anything, but break away from that stress. After all, dressage is meant to be fun. (Figure 3.6)

4 LIGHT AND EASY BASICS

THE AIM FOR a dressage rider is to establish energetic 'free flow' in the gaits, and so vital is this part of the training that dressage could be renamed gait training. In addition to this free flow, balance is involved. Free flow is the energy flowing through the horse's body when in movement, and balance explains the way the horse holds himself within the way of going he uses to utilize this free flow. To establish such qualities the rider must institute the basics, which are so pivotal to dressage, from the beginning to the completion of training, that they have to be thoroughly understood and implemented if success is to be achieved.

The first stage of training these basics is to establish the working gaits of walk, trot, and canter and that the horse moves in balance on a contact, on a long rein, and on a loose rein within these gaits; this is only possible when the horse is in good balance, carries himself, and does not seek support from the reins. The working gaits encourage him to step over the imaginary line delineating his centre of gravity so that the energy powers through, and when the energy created in the horse's hindquarters moves freely through his body to the bit, he shows freedom of expression in the gaits: this is free flow.

Free flow cannot be measured precisely, but it can be seen when the gaits show freedom of expression, and this is always the aim of the dressage rider: to improve the horse's way of going, to improve the walk, trot, and the canter. (Figures 4.1 and 4.2)

Figure 4.1   A nice bouncy canter.

Figure 4.2   Up through the shoulder: good up and forwards movement for the working canter.

Gait Training

Each horse has his own *natural* way of moving, a way special to him that no other horse shows, a forwardness and balance given by Nature. The rider's job is to identify this natural way of going, be sympathetic to it, but to develop it until it mirrors the recognized ways of dressage; for example, the working and collected gaits, and the medium and extended tempos. A trainer knows the horse was not born to be put in a straitjacket of man-made rules and regulations and she opens her heart to the horse and develops the gaits to match his natural way of going until he builds strength and understanding, and grows to meet the requirements laid out over hundreds of years by classical riders, which have been proven to be correct.

A horse must first be observed moving freely in the field, or an enclosed area like a school or arena, where information can be gleaned to help understand the horse's strengths and weaknesses. Ways must then be sought to overcome his weaknesses and to improve his strengths, and particular attention must be paid to the way he uses his body in the walk, trot, and canter. This focus on building up his physical abilities so they can comply with accepted dressage movement results in a dressage horse. In fact, this process happens naturally if the training is followed in a progressive way. It must be appreciated that gait training is the essence of success in dressage and that the measure of a dressage horse is the purity, regularity, correctness and expression of his gaits.

There are a number of exercises that can be carried out to help you understand and improve a horse's gaits.

STUDYING THE GAITS

Bandages exercise

A practical way to understand how the horse moves in the three gaits is to bandage his legs with coloured bandages that correspond to the leg sequences of each gait, i.e. two colours for trot, four for walk, and three for canter. (N.B. Bandage correctly to avoid pressure points.) The sequence of footfalls in each gait can then be clearly seen. This is explained in the table below.

GAIT	SEQUENCE OF FOOTFALLS	BANDAGING THE HORSE'S LEGS TO CORRESPOND TO THE GAITS' FOOTFALLS
WALK	The horse marches each leg forwards in a four-time rhythm so that four hoof beats can be heard, e.g: 1) Right hind leg (outside hind leg) 2) Right foreleg (outside foreleg) 3) Left hind leg (inside hind leg) 4) Left foreleg (inside foreleg) There is no period of suspension in the walk.	Take four different coloured bandages and put one on each leg. Watch the horse moving in walk and count the four-time rhythm at the same time.
TROT	This is a two-time movement, e.g. the horse lifts up his left diagonal pair of legs but shortly before he places them back to the ground he lifts the right diagonal pair off the ground. This means the horse moves with all four legs in the air for a moment of suspension. 1) Left diagonal (the right hind and left fore) 2) Moment of suspension 3) Right diagonal (left hind and right fore) 4) Moment of suspension The trot is regular if the period of time each diagonal is engaged is the same (i.e. lifted, moved forwards, and placed down again).	Take two bandages of the same colour and put them on the left diagonal. Do the same with another two same-colour bandages for the right diagonal. Watch the horse moving in a brisk trot and count the two-time rhythm of the working trot.

| CANTER | The canter can be described as a series of three bounds, a jump-like movement. If you listen to the horse moving in the canter you hear three beats, e.g:
 1) Right hind leg (outside hind leg)
 2) Left hind leg and right foreleg together (inside hind leg and outside foreleg together)
 3) Left foreleg
 4) Moment of suspension. | Take one bandage of one colour, and place it on the outside hind leg. Take two bandages of another colour and place them on the diagonal pair (2nd stride – see left). Now take a third coloured bandage and place it on the inside foreleg. This indicates the leading leg, and so if the last stride of the sequence is made by the inside foreleg, the left foreleg, the horse is moving in left true canter. |

Studying the gaits can be fun. Take a cup of tea into the arena, have a chat with a friend, and observe the horse moving. Test your understanding; a good rider soon picks up the horse's movement like an electronic tracking device! Not only is it fun, it should also be a challenge. It should be possible to identify faults and quality work, differentiate between the two, and to think through ways to improve what is observed. Knowledge soaks into the subconscious and is stored for future riding sessions, and most of this fine tuning relates to gait training; the rider is sensitive to, and inquisitive about, it, and appreciates that it is the crux of dressage.

RECOGNIZING THE FEEL OF THE GAITS

A good way for riders to boost their feel for the gaits is to do the following exercises, which most riders pick up quickly. They are best done with the eyes closed because it heightens feel.

Safety first   These exercises must be performed in a safe environment and preferably while on the lunge, particularly in trot and canter, but if a rider is on a safe, non-spooky horse and has a trainer or friend standing in the middle of a circle in a *small* indoor arena watching the proceedings carefully, they could be performed off the lunge.

The walk

Ride in walk on a circle and close your eyes; feel the four-time rhythm of this gait and count 1-2-3-4 aloud. Next, ask the lunger or observer to say 'now' every time the horse's outside hind leg is placed on the ground. This is continued until you feel confident to take over and say 'now', without any prompting, at precisely the time when the outside hind leg hits the ground. If you make mistakes the observer tells you; you then pick up the exercise again until you have worked out the rhythm of the walk by relying on feel. The exercise is done on both reins.

The trot

As with the walk, the object is for the rider to move in unison with the horse, to know when he is using which legs, and in which order. At this faster gait it is best for the rider to keep her eyes open.

As you ride forwards in rising working trot, the observer again says 'now' every time the outside foreleg is moving back when you are sitting in the saddle, i.e. the horse is moving on the correct diagonal for the rein he is working on and you are doing the down part of the *up-down* of the rising trot. This feeling will be assimilated so that you will automatically know when you are riding on the correct diagonal. If you ride on the incorrect diagonal, however, the observer will explain this to you as it happens. Correcting it will help you identify and develop a feel for riding on the correct diagonal. It is quite common for riders to be scratchy about knowing whether or not they are on the correct diagonal, but once this simple exercise is done it becomes easy.

Follow the above exercise with sitting for a few strides in upward transitions from walk to trot, and get the feel of rising out the saddle at the correct moment to be riding on the correct diagonal for the correct rein. In fact, rising trot is usually executed sandwiched between a few strides of sitting trot but many riders form the habit of constantly riding rising trot without these interim steps of sitting trot. The only time it is acceptable to rise instantly is on a young horse when it softens the effects of the rider's weight.

This part of the exercise is helpful for establishing rider seat stability, and feel for riding on the correct diagonal.

Most riders find the exercise in trot is easier than the walk, but it is safer not to progress to trot until you have mastered the slower exercise.

The canter

The canter exercise is more advanced than those for walk and trot and is normally started when the horse is working in collected canter. However, it can be started on the lunge in working canter if the horse has a naturally good canter and a rider feels happy to do so in a safe environment as already discussed. *It must only be ridden with the eyes open, unless a rider has the confidence to ride it with the eyes closed while being lunged by a competent handler.*

This gait can be divided into three parts: the first step, the middle where the diagonal set of legs moves through, and the 'top' of the canter when the leading leg moves forwards. Firstly, aim to feel the first step of the canter, i.e. the engagement of the outside hind leg, and it is best done in walk-to-canter transitions to get the feel for this engagement. This time, the 'now' instruction comes from the observer when this outside hind leg is on the ground. Once you can feel that first part of the three-time rhythm of the canter, advance to feeling the top of the canter. The first step is easy to feel in walk to canter: a sinking down of the hindquarters comes through the seat. The middle part flows through automatically, but the discriminating part of the canter stride is that of the leading leg reaching forward where the energy flows through the horse's back up to the front of the saddle. This energy flow can be felt as it comes up to the front of the saddle.

In order for you to learn to feel the top of the canter, the observer must say, 'now' every time it happens and then, again, you take over, with the observer pointing out when you make a mistake. If you sit quietly, let the canter flow through, and feel the movement with your seat, you will soon pick up on this stride sequence. It is useful to be able to feel the top of the canter especially when starting collected canter, and for balancing the canter through half-halts for transitions to trot and to tidy the canter for canter to walk, or to tone down exuberant strides. In these instances, keep the leg relaxed not increasing the pressure for that split second when the energy comes up through the seat, but half-halt with the hand in the top part of the canter stride sequence. It sounds complicated, but start with being able to discern the first steps of the canter stride sequence, and practise steadily, you will soon pick it up.

If you are unable to do this exercise either because the horse is not advanced enough in the canter work, or the horse is too lively on the lunge, you can start with preliminary canter-feel exercises by asking your observer to count out the strides in 1, 2, 3 rhythm, like counting in time to music. The rider then takes over until she is able to synchronize the correct three-time beat with that of her horse.

IMPROVING THE GAITS

The obvious exercises such as riding transitions, circles and figure work are done, but below I have added extra information that I hope you will find helpful.

The walk

Walk is a wonderful gait for collecting a horse's thoughts, calming his mental processes, and for suppling and toning his body.

Walk gives horses time to think through new exercises; they don't have to worry about their legs knocking each other. Young horses in particular have legs that seem to move like elastic bands, and they often worry about hurting themselves or where they are placing their feet, especially in new exercises. It is like eating spaghetti, once you have the technique, nothing can be easier. Walk gives the horse time to get conditioned to the sequence of footfalls; it builds confidence.

Walk is also good for the composure of both horse and rider. It seems like nothing is happening, yet suppleness and posture are improved, confidence gained, and obedience boosted. Surprisingly, the walk is often neglected but, providing it is ridden actively forwards without rushing and disrupting the four-time rhythm, it is an excellent training gait. Here are some benefits.

- The walk calms a hot horse, and used over a period of time can settle even the most nervous horse. A hot horse is often hot-blooded and highly strung, whereas a fresh-tempered horse is lively but with a less hot character. Once a hot horse is calm, trot can be added, but canter is best left until he has settled right down. This may happen during one training session, over several weeks or, in unusual cases, even months.

- The young feisty horse will often be fresh rather than hot, and such a horse is best ridden forward at a brisk trot first before the calming walk work.
- A rider should be careful to keep the walk energetic. For a young horse a gentle tap on the shoulder with a short stick is better than prodding continuously with the legs. In fact, overuse of the legs in walk is to be avoided; the horse is in walk after all, not in gallop. The rider wants to be able to sit quietly and, with minimum effort, to encourage the walk forwards. This is often best done by simply riding with a *very soft seat* to follow the forward and back movement (see page 38) This movement comes up through the saddle as the horse takes longer walk steps. If the horse still resists walking forwards actively, transitions to trot can be added to freshen up the walk. Also, hacking out a horse who is lazy in the walk with a horse who walks out actively is a good way to improve a poor walk.
- If the walk lacks energy the rider can use walk-to-canter transitions; these two gaits are closely connected. Often a good racehorse will be seen to overtrack well in the walk, and the synchronization of the leg sequences in walk and canter work well together, giving each other a boost in energy.
- You can insert periods of walk into walk-to-canter work in order to calm a fizzy horse down after the hotting up of the canter. This routine will also keep a lazy horse on his toes and give him a punchier walk.
- The overtracking of the walk strides can be improved by joining lots of trot-to-walk and walk-to-trot transitions to walking over ground poles. Approach the poles in trot and ride forwards to walk just before the poles, going over them in walk and riding forwards to an active trot after the poles. This exercise is best done in a figure-of-eight with the poles placed in the centre of the arena and performed on both reins.
- Free walk on a long or loose rein (see below) has many advantages and can be encouraged by the trainer walking next to the horse or by the rider (Figure 4.3).

 a) It allows the horse to stretch the muscles after work on the bridle.

Figure 4.3   The trainer can walk beside a horse to encourage him to walk on a long rein. Here we see the horse stretching so that his withers are level with his ears; this is sufficient for many horses and the stretching down exercise can be ridden as a separate exercise at a different time.

b) It gives him time to rest and regain his composure.
c) It offers a peaceful time for the rider to re-evaluate the next exercise to be done in a schooling session.
d) It adds zest to the energy of the walk without rushing or overriding this gait, and has overcome the drawbacks of the walk having no suspension: the rider always being aware that lack of suspension makes the walk vulnerable to faults of lack of engagement. This is the opposite of that which the dressage rider wants from a dressage horse.

In addition to the above points, the walk acts as a breathing period, a break between bursts of trot and canter work that require more stamina. It is important to intersperse all training sessions with frequent short periods (of just a few minutes at a time) of free walk on a loose rein (or long rein). Sometimes this seems impossible with an eager horse, but if you ask gently from active work on a long rein with slightly more contact than normal, and by conditioning over a period of time you will find you can lighten this feel to a genuine walk on a long rein to walk on a loose rein. Sometimes it is simply a case of the horse understanding that you do not want too much, that it is perfectly acceptable to go along quietly in free walk on a long rein. A horse enjoys being allowed to have the time to stretch and relax.

If a horse has been pushed too aggressively through the training scales it can result in a jog-walk and it takes patience to unravel the incorrectly trained basics, but using free walk on a long rein out hacking over periods of time (sometimes months) adds a dimension to the work. Used intelligently it can work miracles and turn even the most agitated horse into a calm easy-going character. It is often just a matter of trust: there has to be one rider who is kind enough to show trust in, and care for, the horse to give him that time to progress steadily and, if mistakes have been made, to unravel them, and start again. Such a horse always rewards a generous rider in a spectacular way, by breathing sighs of relief and saying, in effect: 'OK, I'm not going anywhere fast, and this rider is not hassling me so I'll relax and walk on a long rein.' In other words, he lets go, his muscles relax, the tension goes, and good work will soon follow. It is better to persevere and be patient with such a horse; he will often have a lot of talent but, as stated, just needs the right rider.

Faults to avoid in the walk
A rider must ensure that there is enough energy, that the gait is not too slow or lacking activity. When riding on a contact rein there must be a light feel; when riding on a long rein there is still a feel, still a contact, with the horse's mouth; and when riding on a loose rein the reins can be held at the buckle, the only weight should be that of the reins with no weight coming from the rider's hands.

Signs of tension are:
1. Dragging feet, or running faster instead of stepping through purposefully.
2. Becoming tight on the rein, which indicates the rider's hands are too strong.
3. An incorrect head carriage; for example: the horse tips his head lower on one side than the other, or there is too much energy for the horse's balance and he falls on to his forehand or scrunches his lips up in disgust as if to spit out the bit.

4. Coming behind the bit.
5. Becoming unsteady in the mouth when he was always steady beforehand, i.e. over-chewing the bit, clenching the bit in his mouth or clamping on to one side of the bit.

Periods of walk on a loose rein will often sort out these faults, together with active periods of trot and canter work. A rider must be aware that a lack of suspension in the walk exaggerates the fault of a lack of energy coming through to the bridle, which will be felt as faulty contact. It can also feel like the walk is moving back towards the seat rather than forwards from it. Dropping the contact onto a loose rein automatically solves such problems because the horse can step freely forward over the line of the centre of gravity and regain his own balance rather than propping himself on the rein. Faults in the walk can often be traced to incorrect contact and so I emphasize that walk on a long and/or loose rein can cure so many problems in this gait.

The trot

Trot is the athletic gait and helps dressage training in a unique way; unlike the other two gaits it is symmetrical. It is a two-time movement with natural energy and spring, and the energy moves more equally through both sides of the horse's body than with the walk or canter, even before the horse has been properly straightened through dressage training. It gives the rider opportunities to improve activity, to achieve acceptance of the contact equally on both sides of the bit and the stepping through from the hind leg with straightness and engagement. (Figure 4.4) All trots can be improved beyond expectations, even a poor trot being gradually made better by steady application of gymnastic dressage training.

Besides the trot's actual two-time rhythm and its propensity for equal energy distribution, the spring in the trot steps themselves combined with the moment of suspension sandwiched between each diagonal boosts training in a spectacular way, the very effervescence of the energy enhancing the horse's desire for forward momentum. The rider tunes into this dimension. Used intelligently, the trot can enhance all three gaits by the development of the throughness and this brings better swing coming through into the transitions.

Figure 4.4   The working trot is a brisk trot; a trot with more energy than the horse does naturally. It is the foundation of all dressage work and needs to be established before collection can be started. It also acts as a refresher within other work to boost the energy and bring the horse more actively forward to the bit.

Trot exercises

- Emphasis should be put on transition work: walk to trot, trot to walk and trot to canter and canter to trot, and progressing to halt to trot and, lastly, trot to halt. More details on transition work are given in the transition section in this chapter.

- Flexions to the inside and outside soften and engage the horse around the rider's inside leg, and connects him to the outside rein (see Chapter 5).

- Different school figures should be used for variety and to supple both sides of the horse's body through his ribs, which in turn helps straightness and working through to the rein.

- Rising trot can be used to ensure that the diagonals step through equally from behind to the bridle and each diagonal step is of equal length. It is best to focus on rising trot until the horse is well strengthened in trot work, only using short periods of sitting trot between transitions.

- When commenced, sitting trot should continue to be performed for short periods only between sessions of rising trot. Once it is established – providing the rider keeps her seat soft and alive with the movement of the horse – the extra weight of the sitting-trot seat helps to build up the muscles of the horse's back; it has the same effect as the weights lifted by a body builder.

- A springy trot on a circle can help a fresh horse step through. This trot should be active but not quite a working trot with the horse moving in a rounded outline to the bit. This way of going keeps him contained and obedient and reduces his desire to rush off in too quick a rhythm and avoiding stepping through his back, resulting in him pinging off his legs rather than the energy working through his body, which is the opposite of what the dressage rider wants, but this type of trot work works the horse through his back into the rider's hand. The energy travels up through his withers, neck and poll and then on to the bit, bringing the horse into a round outline. The rider can now apply the leg aids and ask the horse to step more actively forwards to the bridle. The trot flows through the top-line muscles and boosts the purity of the gait.

  Using lateral work enhances the cleanness of the trot gait adding spring and dimension to the diagonalization.

- Exercises in self-carriage are best begun in the trot because the steadiness of this gait, and its way of moving allows the horse to keep his balance easily. This gives him the best opportunity to maintain rhythm and contact steadily through the self-carriage.

Faults to avoid in trot

- If the trot shuffles instead of stepping actively forwards the rider applies the legs to ask for a forward reaction. If the horse *rushes* forward, trotting with quick sewing-machine type steps, he must be rebalanced with forward asking aids, using transitions and half-halts, to refresh the energy, without too much speed. Speed does not equal activity; the rider wants big strides, not lots of little quick-moving ones. She can also slow the rhythm down by slowing the energy flowing through her seat so that the horse picks up on this change and follows it. She may need to back it up with give and take feels on the outside rein, but she

Figure 4.5   Working through the trot, which lacks activity.

should ask with the seat first, and only use the hand aids if necessary.

- If there is not enough energy, the horse will fail to pick his feet up practically dragging his feet along the surface of the arena (Figure 4.5).

- The contact will become heavy if there is more energy than the horse can sustain and still remain in balance. The rider half halts, and/or balances the horse through transition work, and rides forwards through this renewed balance into a steady hand.

- The diagonals of the trot should not appear to run into each other; each diagonal should be clean-cut, and separately defined. Again, supple the horse through riding figures, transitions, and lateral work, to overcome these problems.

- When the horse lacks free forward flow it often points to stiffness (often in the shoulders, and/or hindquarters); suppling exercises such as figure riding or lateral work also put these faults right. Stoking up the energy is not always the answer because if the shoulders are stiff the horse will just run faster with shorter quicker steps, but if the shoulders are suppled it allows the energy to move through the body.

Figures 4.6a and b   Simple pole work and jumping exercises, providing they are done with care, can encourage throughness, and bring an added interest for horses that like jumping.

The canter

There are many things that can be done to establish and improve the canter.

- Ground-pole work can encourage engagement and working through (Figures 4.6a and b).
- Trot-to-canter transitions are superb for rounding up the horse so that the muscles of the back synchronize with each other and the energy is freed up.
- Walk-to-canter transitions help the canter elevation and the power to come through (Figure 4.7). It keeps the stability of the canter in the hand and seems to help the horse organize himself in this asymmetrical gait. (Figures 4.8a–c)
- Suspension in the canter can carry the horse through this tendency to crookedness and can be improved by the rider using transitions within the gait to rev up the power; for example, collected canter to medium canter and a neater working canter to strong working canter, and combining these transitions within the gait with sessions of walk-to-canter

transitions synchronizes the horse's footfalls in both gaits and improves the canter.

- Keep the canter active and forward, i.e. a strong working canter. However, some horses like to move in a neat canter, a canter that tends towards collection, and if this is the case, let the horse work in this neat canter rather than pushing him beyond his balance. Once he is strengthened and has regained his confidence, the rider will be able to develop a standard working canter.

Figure 4.7   Up and forward, cantering with joy.

- Combine working canter with collected canter and add walk-to-canter and canter-to-walk transitions. Small amounts of reining back interspersed with this work further boosts bounce in the canter. Give the horse periods of rest on a loose rein when you do this work.

- Riding working canter to stronger working canter, to medium canter, and then small amounts of collected canter, helps freshen up the activity and jump in the canter strides.

- Work on walk-straightening exercises (see Chapter 6) helps the canter. The rider supples the connection of the front and back of the horse and as a result the horse will be more obedient to the hand and straighter.

- Some horses get a little gung ho when cantering (Figure 4.9). A rider needs to understand that only when the horse is relaxed can the muscles be suppled; working a horse with tense muscles can make him muscle bound. If a horse gets too frisky and charges off in the canter, introduce lots of slowing transitions, such as trot to canter, followed by steady periods of active neat trot work that is not too extravagant and do this work on the circle. Rest periods on a loose or long rein in walk will also help. It is good that the horse is keen to move forwards and the rider must

Figures 4.8a–c a) Active canter but the rider's hands are fixed and the horse is tense through the back. b) Melissa makes the correction with a slight giving of the inside rein towards the horse's mouth, and in c) we see the results of the corrected riding with the canter fuller and the horse becoming softer in the poll, coming to the bit more and working more up through the back.

not stifle this reaction but temper it with intelligent riding so that it is controllable.

- The canter is normally developed after the trot and walk are well established, but it increases in importance as the dressage training advances. Eventually it can take up over a third

Figure 4.9   Sometimes horses get a little carried away when cantering and scoot off.

of the exercising session. This dedication to the canter training normally starts sooner with a show-jumper. However, because of the asymmetrical nature of the canter the dressage rider is conservative about ploughing on too soon with such concentrated canter work. The time for the canter to grow in importance for the dressage horse is at about Medium level, depending on each individual horse, his character, and his natural ability in the canter. If he loves, and has a good, canter, it can be developed prior to this level, but he must be given plenty of rest periods to ensure he is not stressed or strained.

- The horse needs more respiratory fitness to canter continuously and this must be developed gradually to avoid physical problems or mental stress. Be generous and err on the side of the horse; give him a chance to come to his training at the pace that suits him.

Because the canter is asymmetrical, a rider must focus on getting it straight before advancing too much with this gait; if she advances without paying enough attention to straightening, the quality will be inferior. Again, the rider uses figure work, and suppling exercises, but she also has at her disposal the **counter-canter**, an exercise peculiar to the canter when the horse is cantered with the leading leg on the opposite side to the direction of movement. It is very good for straightening the horse because it supples and bends the horse through the diagonal phase of the canter, i.e. the second stride of the canter.

Two exercises for introducing counter-canter

1. The horse is ridden straight along the quarter or three-quarter line and is asked for walk to counter-canter or trot to counter-canter along this line, coming forward to trot or walk before the corner. Once the horse is familiar with the exercise, extra transitions can be ridden along the long side; for example, a few steps of trot to counter-canter followed by a few steps of trot to true canter. When the horse is happy counter-cantering along the straight lines of the arena, a few counter-canter steps around the corner can be introduced. When the horse is comfortable with this exercise, ask for a few more steps of counter-canter, a few at a time, until he can keep his balance in counter-canter around the entire corner (this can take 6–12 months). Keep the horse alert to the aids so that he does not know if he is going to be asked for true canter or counter-canter. The exercises increase in difficulty gradually. Some horses get upset with counter-canter because when they have only been asked for true canter in an arena, they feel they are being punished. But if the work is taken slowly a horse will stay relaxed and the progress will be steady and good. Generally most horses find it easy, and it is just a matter of practice.

2) A second easy exercise for introducing counter-canter is to ride a teardrop shape. The horse is ridden in true canter going large moving onto a 15 m half circle at the top end of the school. Once the half circle is completed, position him onto a straight line back towards the track he has been working on. Keep a very slight bend towards the leading leg, place the leg on softly on the side of the bend and keep a steady outside rein. When you arrive at the track, the horse will be in counter-canter.

Some horses panic when they find themselves in counter-canter along the track because the worry about the perimeters of the arena. For such a horse, position the exercise slightly in from the track and then he will see there is nothing to worry about and his confidence in the counter-canter exercises will grow.

However, if the horse still frets, return to the previous exercise until he is happy to canter or counter-canter on the inside line of the track. Gradually bring this work closer to the track, and eventually onto the track. Many horses seem to prefer this exercise to the teardrop exercise and a rider must use the exercise that best suits her horse. (Figures 4.10a–d) Counter-canter across the diagonal should only be performed when the horse is proficient in both the above exercises because, not only is it more difficult, but horses who have a naturally good canter may also start to flick in flying changes of lead rather than remaining in counter-canter.

Faults to avoid in canter
A rider will know if a horse is stiff in the canter because he will find it difficult to hold the canter strides, or he will run in trot with the forelegs and slop along in the canter with the hind legs. Transition work corrects these problems: for example, bouncy canter – a canter that feels as if the horse could spring into a lovely big jump after each canter stride – worked into a strong working canter boosts the energy, and dispels slackness in the gait. The increased power carried through the period of suspension in the canter seems to iron out stiffness through this freedom in the gait – the actual 'bounce' travelling up and giving the gait a wonderful 'air' of its own.

Suppling exercises such as shoulder-fore in walk are useful as are trot-to-canter transitions going large.

Be careful the canter does not degenerate into a four-time rhythm, which will turn it into a lollop rather than a canter. The gait must be ridden forwards actively and briskly.

In fact, simple trot-to-canter and canter-to-trot transitions often prove the best way to sort out problems in the canter, and always add to the quality of the work.

WORKING ON THE GAITS SEPARATELY
You would normally use the three gaits in each training session, but sometimes it is better to work on each one separately, or just two together; for example, the walk and trot together, or the walk and canter.

Each gait has benefits peculiar to the way the horse uses his body, and you

Figures 4.10a–d a) Counter-canter exercises encourage the horse to move to both sides of the bit equally and to move straight, and are good exercises for straightening the canter and for getting a better acceptance of the bridle in this gait. b) True canter. c) Counter-canter along the long side and d) counter canter across the diagonal. Counter-canter can be begun once the horse is established in the working canter. Start by riding simple counter-canter across the diagonal, because only a few steps are required and it does not over-tax the horse. Never counter-canter around the corner until the horse is balanced in this exercise, and progress to counter-canter along the long side. See the text for more advice on riding counter-canter. Normally the counter-canter exercise is started following work on canter loops and is ridden for just a few strides along the long side. Then the exercise can be ridden along the ¾ and ¼ lines, for a few strides around a corner, working up to counter-cantering round the whole of a short side of the arena and along the long side of the arena. Take it steady and progress when the horse is happy with the easier exercises. With counter-canter the horse canters with the leading leg to the outside and this is more difficult and confusing for novice riders than for the horse. Build up your confidence by riding counter-canter on the ¼ and ¾ lines without riding it around the corner and you should find it easy. Start with trot to counter-canter, although some riders find it easier to go from walk into the transition.

can use each one for different purposes: to develop one gait, or to hitch it to another gait to get better throughness and suppleness, but the natural propensity of each gait together with its own dimensions will give clues as to which exercises, and which gait, to use to get the desired effects. This need not get too technical, but you should be aware of the benefits of each gait.

- **The walk** promotes suppleness, calmness, muscle tone/posture, and aids relaxation of the muscles.
- **The trot** improves contact, throughness, straightness, and aids gymnastic development.
- **The canter** boosts fitness, tones up the horse's stomach muscles. The topline is suppled and the horse becomes more rounded, which produces better contact. Canter exercises improves respiratory fitness. When combined with walk and trot, the canter encourages the energy to travel through to the mouth better.

TIPS ON THE GAITS

The gaits are fixed to the horse's urge to move forwards. He was born to move for sixteen hours a day when he lived in the wild, and this desire is still strong in him. Horses love to move, stifling this urge makes them unhappy. You never see a lazy horse in the field, he is never lazy if he wants to play, and the wise dressage rider taps into this delight of moving forwards. This natural desire to use energy is an expression of the horse's character and makes him more beautiful, and a rider streamlines this desire to move forwards into the direction she has decided – it is harnessed into contained energy. This is the essence of dressage.

This natural energy being used by a rider can be likened to a sailing yacht being moved forwards by the wind blowing into its sails: it is not man but nature that creates the wind. This same phenomenon occurs in the horse with his natural desire to move forwards, and the wise rider taps into this natural desire.

Training must improve the gaits. If your horse's gaits do not improve after six months training give the trainer the sack! Well, perhaps not too quickly, but understand that improving the gaits is the beginning and end of dressage work, and all the movements and exercises are developed to this end.

Transitions

Transitions kick-start the development of free flow; they act as a bridge between the hindquarters and the forehand of the horse and are the ultimate tool for training. The thinking rider aims to ride plenty of transitions every schooling session because they improve balance and make it easier to achieve success. Good transitions are the foundations of quality dressage training encouraging better balance and improving a horse's way of going. Once you can ride good transitions, you will continue to strive for better ones, knowing the work will get better and better. Transitions come in different categories.

Upward transitions   The horse moves up from a lower to a higher gait, e.g. halt to walk, walk to trot, and trot to canter.

Downward transitions   The horse moves down from a higher to a lower gait, e.g. canter to trot, trot to walk and walk to halt

Transitions within the gaits   The horse moves up or down in tempo within each gait, e.g. working to medium trot, working to medium canter, free walk on a long rein to medium walk.

Half transitions   The horse *almost* moves up or down from one gait to another, seemingly taking a pause between each gait and being suspended in this pause. These half transitions (especially the trot to near-walk [i.e. the point of nearly walking] and then stepping forwards to trot again) are preparatory exercises for half-halts and aid balance and collection.

Transitions *must* move forward; banish the word '*backward*' from the dressage vocabulary (*especially* when riding transitions) – always think forward, always ride forward into forwards-upwards transitions and forwards-downwards transitions.

Always think **forwards within the balance.** Never create more energy than you can hold in the hand, or restrict it coming through, otherwise you unbalance the horse, letting him fall onto his forehand, or restrict the freedom of the gaits.

Transitions are progressive or direct. When they are **progressive** they are ridden forwards downwards, or forwards upwards, in a gradual, active, progressive way that gives the horse *time to step under with his hind legs* in an active way so that he steps *through* his back (i.e. he engages his hind legs and the energy moves forwards, through his body and over the line of his centre of gravity; this energy rounds his topline). **Direct** transitions are still ridden actively forwards but there is more bending of the horse's hind-leg joints, and they cover such transitions as halt to trot and walk to canter. This work requires a greater degree of suppleness, therefore it is used for more developed horses and even then the direct transitions will be sandwiched between progressive ones. This guideline covers Novice to Advanced horses, the progressive transitions refreshing the gaits and the direct ones giving better balance and elevation of the forehand.

Transitions should be ridden smoothly to *avoid blocking the free flow* so that it is *taken forward through the horse's body in a streamlined manner*. Over a period of time the resulting suppleness will reverberate throughout his musculature system, joints and sinews. The muscles along his topline – including the muscles over his withers, along his neck, and over his poll – will ripple like wheat rippling in the breeze.

To sum up the guidelines for riding transitions:

a) 'Progressive' is a classical expression that applies to the working gaits and describes steady, forwards and gentle transitions that put little strain on the horse. Use them for young or novice horses, or for warming up schooled horses. They act as a primer for the more serious work for the more advanced horse, but for novice horses progressive transitions in the working gaits are used almost exclusively.

b) Direct transitions, collected and extended tempos, are worked into the training over a period of time.

In both progressive and direct transitions the horse must be active forwards to the contact and relaxed in a supple way through his body.

TRANSITION EXERCISES

Walk transitions

Halt to walk and walk to halt brings the horse to the hand and promotes quick and easy reactions to all the aids. Being a slow gait, walk gives horse and rider time to think through what is happening, the rider can be systematic in the application of the aids and feel instant results as the horse responds clearly and in a calm manner as he walks forward in this slow moving, almost hypnotic gait.

These transitions are especially helpful for young novice horses. It makes them wait for direction from the rider instead of barging off on their own course and, providing the reins are held lightly and sensitively while using medium walk, they tone the muscles and bring good posture. You must be very careful to intersperse such work on a contact rein with active trot or canter transitions, or with walk on a long or loose rein so that energy in the walk is preserved.

To ride the upward transition sit taller and squeeze with the calf muscles or, if the horse responds to light aids, put more weight on both stirrups and, at the same time, hold the same contact. These riding techniques are explained in Chapter 2. Sometimes it helps a young horse if you quietly ease the hand towards the horse's mouth a few inches for a few strides but, as explained in Chapter 5, you must be careful to reconnect the horse to the contact.

Once the horse is walking freely forwards, allow your hips to follow the movement of the walk in a supple way like jelly on a plate; the jelly sticks to the plate yet is relatively fluid in its composition, and your seat should also move fluidly with the movement coming through the horse's back in walk. You will feel a forward and back movement coming through your seat; while keeping your upper body upright your hips move independently.

To ride the downward transition, stop the movement through the hips and allow it to come up to the pommel of the saddle. You will feel a lifting up through the ribs in the last stride of the walk. If it has been timed well, the horse will stop as the movement stops because he will be following your body movement looking for support from the body placement.

Normally, these seat actions are enough to get walk-to-halt transitions, and it is better that they are ridden with just the use of the seat. Once the horse is working well on the seat aids, light half-halts can be used on the rein to prompt the halt and keep better balance in the hand. When these transitions secure the halt, the young horse often benefits from a very light softening of your hand on the side of the bit on which he may stiffen so that both sides of the horse come to the halt equally. These aids must be applied discreetly with no pulling back on the reins towards the hips, but with a forward-thinking hand.

Trot transitions

Walk-to-trot and trot-to-walk transitions are the first easy activating steps you use to bring the horse to gymnastic fitness and forwardness. At Preliminary and Novice level they are best ridden progressively, i.e. in a natural balanced way that allows the horse to step actively over the line of his centre of gravity by overtracking. This type of active progressive transition increases the bend of the hind-leg joints and promotes engagement in preparation for the half-halt work and collection.

'Progressive' means the horse is ridden forwards so that the energy comes through actively from behind and there is increased bending of the hind legs and increased overtracking. When riding these transitions a young horse often requires at least 10 strides of medium walk before he regains the balance to move forward in trot. Gradually his balance improves and the number of walk steps sandwiched between the trot work diminishes to 5 strides, to 4, to 3, and so on. Once this stage is reached direct transitions of halt to trot and trot to halt are started. But you should still use progressive transitions in every schooling session to freshen up the forwardness of the trot and to keep the free flow moving freely through the horse's body. They ensure the riding is not blocking the horse's ability for free forward movement. Also, she may keep using rising trot in this progressive transition work even when the horse is well established, and only adopt sitting trot once he is thoroughly worked through his back and rounding up through his topline to the movement.

To ride the upward transitions, as with the walk transitions, sit taller, stretch the legs down putting slightly more weight on the stirrups and squeeze with the calf muscles, but if there is no response give a tap with your heels to nudge the horse forward. Keep the rein contact the same, but if you have previously been riding in walk you may have to adjust the reins for the new trot gait. You will soon know which length of rein suits your horse for whichever gait and tempo he is working in. Keep the elbows supple as you hold the contact steady, and if your horse does not move briskly forwards, ease your elbows slightly towards the horse's mouth for a few strides to allow and encourage him to go forward.

Feel the different beat of the trot from that of the walk or canter – it is more of a 1-2 bouncy movement. By absorbing this movement through your hips you can allow the energy to flow through more, and letting this movement come through helps to collect the gait and bring out the expression of medium and extended tempos. In the working tempo the feeling in the seat is forward and backward rather than up and down, as is often taught. It is easy to feel the differences in your seat and you can alternate between the more horizontal forward-and-back movement with the hips in sitting trot for the medium and extended tempos and the more vertical up-and-down movement for the collected tempo but you must always be aware of these rhythm changes in your hips.

Remember that all good dressage riding comes from the hips, either moving with the horse, or using them against the movement to stop the forward momentum. Once the power in the seat is understood, it is possible to gradually teach the horse to respond more and more to these tiny differences in the hip movements. It helps if you think of your seat bones as the tops of your legs, i.e. your backside is an extension of your legs, and be aware that your seat bones lie close to the horse's back. This explains why good dressage riders have mastered such riding techniques as the sitting trot to a fine degree.

To ride the downward transitions in rising trot and on a young horse, the forward and backs (or up-downs) of the rises simply need to be reduced. The horse will be guided by your seat, always wanting to align his centre of gravity with yours, and he will reduce his trot strides for a downward transition. Initially, the seat gives enough direction to the horse because it is best that he is just ridden forward in this downward transition to ensure that the energy is not blocked. Once forwardness is established, however, you can use half-halts combined with the seat and leg directions. The half-halts are normally applied with the outside rein only because this rein is used to ask for changes of speed, but often both reins are used to encourage straightness. Use the inside rein on its own if this is a horse's stiff rein and he tends to hang on it, but be discreet with it; use it solely for this purpose and only for a limited period of time.

Halt-to-trot and trot-to-halt transitions are begun at Novice stage when the horse is stepping through well in the progressive transitions of walk to trot and trot to walk. They give you a means to increase engagement. Ensure the energy is flowing through well if you want to get all the benefit of this work. In the upward transition, ask the horse to move briskly forwards off the leg aids without hesitation into the new gait.

Canter transitions

Trot to canter is normally the first canter transition taught to the horse. You must be specific about your instructions: the inside seat bone should be weighted more, the inside leg stretched down more to the inside stirrup and the inside calf muscle applied (a gentle nudge with the heel works wonders if the horse is resistant to the lighter aid). The outside leg *can* be positioned softly behind the girth as the initial aid, a type of indicator light to the horse that canter is about to happen, but you must be careful with novice horses because they can get upset with the outside leg aid and either scoot off or pick up the wrong leading leg in canter. This is often, but not always, the case but if you do use the outside leg with a novice horse, slide it quietly forwards after the upward transition to make sure you are not pressing with this outside leg and making the horse swing his quarters inside the line of the movement of the canter.

Hold the hands in a central position. This is helped by holding the little fingers closer together and not wide apart as is seen in the modern 'side-rein hand' because the classically held hand does not block the forwardness travelling through the horse's back to his mouth. Also, some horses like the hands held a little higher than they would be in the trot because it helps their balance and they feel more comfortable. But these variations of hand position are a matter of feel and cannot be dissected in a scientific way. There are some horses who go better in a wider-held and/or lower-held rein, but in the canter you must be very discreet about using a side-rein hand for the reasons explained above. There is nothing so upsetting to the horse's balance than being held in an unfeeling fixed rigid hand, and the side-rein hand tends to do this unless a rider is careful. The canter bounds forward and the horse needs more freedom in his head and neck to stay balanced and a classically held rein allows for these adjustments quickly and easily. Check that the horse is on the outside rein once the canter is moving forwards by softening that rein because you may have asked for a slight position to the inside as the canter aid and you want to be sure he does not drop onto the inside rein.

Also, riding him up to the outside rein encourages straightness in the canter. If you are in doubt use frequent give and takes on the inside rein to make sure you are not blocking the canter and to ensure the horse is connected to the outside rein. These gentle half-halt aids are best left until the horse reacts forwards and upwards *just* from the different aids of the seat, i.e. the trot seat rather than the canter seat. This downward canter to trot is subtle yet direct because it cuts directly over the horse's centre of gravity and really makes an impression on him. He moves forwards to the trot from the canter without *any* hand aids at all and thus does not fear any restriction, which encourages him to feel free in this simple basic aid. Once he steps through *powerfully* more dimensions of the half-halt aids can be introduced, combining these gentle whisper-like aids on the reins with a gentle bracing of the back. If however you feel any reticence from the horse to step through forwards and downwards in this transition apply the lower leg forward-asking aids discreetly.

Adopt the new rhythm of the new canter gait with your seat once it gets going, but for one stride keep your seat still to absorb the new feel in your seat in order to steady the horse on the new aid and into the canter. Feel the three strides of the canter: the first stride is a sinking down of the hips, the second stride is a following through of the movement, and the third stride feels like a lifting up to the front of the saddle.

When **riding the downward transition, canter to trot,** instigate the feel in your seat to anticipate the two-time rhythm of the trot while the horse is still cantering in that gait's three-time rhythm. Quickly the horse looks for your new balance and understands you want trot.

When he is comfortable with these simple canter-to-trot aids and powering through from behind, you can apply gentle half-halts – almost whispers of half-halts – on the outside rein to back up the normal seat and upper body aids of refreshed half-halt aids. You may find it useful when you first ride this exercise to physically lift your seat a few inches out the saddle at the moment your seat is sitting in the third phase of the canter stride, i.e. when the leading foreleg comes forward because this encourages the horse to move his legs into the two-time trot. That third phase is the best moment to nudge the horse into a change of gait; the top of the canter suiting the seat directions best.

The **walk-to-canter** transition gives engagement of the hind leg, aids collection, and helps balance and spring in the canter strides. Walk and canter work taught together help calm a hot horse from boiling up in the canter. These transitions strengthen the throughness of the energy over the back, improve the walk and its engagement, and increase collection in the canter. Walk-to-canter transitions are normally started after trot-to-canter transitions are performed in good balance, but sometimes they are useful for helping a young horse who struggles with understanding the canter aids because the walk and canter are more closely related in leg synchronization than the trot. A recently born foal on his first outing in a field will walk, canter and frisk around but for some reason he keeps trot as a separate 'air', loving to feel the beauty of each gait's movement and how they work together.

In fact, it was common practice on the continent to teach big young warmbloods walk to canter before trot to canter because they just find it easier to understand the aids, and the rider finds it easier to apply the aids. Normally canter and trot transitions are taught first but it is good to be open-minded about these rules. Sometimes you just need initially to try to establish if walk to canter suits your horse. My advice is to follow the normal trot-to-canter transition first, but be flexible; if you encounter any resistances it is better to return to the classical way of teaching trot-to-canter and canter-to-trot transitions. These transitions are wonderful for bringing the horse through his back so that the energy ripples through his back especially in the muscles behind the saddle, and are a wonderful warming up exercise for young and mature horses.

The aids for walk-to-canter transitions are the same as those for trot to canter with the following subtle differences. The inside seat bone is pressed down as the inside leg is applied and the seat bone and leg aids 'lift' with the lift of the first canter stride as you feel the engagement of the outside hind leg and the lifting of the forehand in the canter. The upper body is positioned very slightly behind the vertical for a few strides. A split second before applying the above aids, the outside leg is positioned 2–3 in (5–7.5 cm) behind the girth putting the knee more into the saddle flap and then gently sliding it forward again so that it does not press against the horse's sides but brushes his coat in a soft caress. Once the horse is in canter, return the upper body to the vertical line and feel the canter strides through your seat. You may find you need to check the activity of the canter with inside leg reminder aids, but be careful not to do this every stride or you are in danger of nagging the horse. In fact, leave it as long as you dare. With a young horse this can be every 3–5 strides but with a more established horse you can, providing he is on the aids, dispense with the leg aids once he is cantering, and instead press your inside seat bone into the saddle as a 'leg reminder'. Remember to think of the seat bones as the top of your legs; in effect the seat bones are your legs. As stated in the riding section, the seat bones are closer to the horse's body and the more refined your riding becomes together with the development of the horse's balance, the more the horse responds to the seat-bone aids and the legs play a lesser role. There is less possibility for incorrect application of the seat-bone aids and so it makes life simpler and easier, resulting in a happier horse and rider.

A rider must be flexible; each horse is different and may require different ways of riding within a schooling session, or over periods of time. The guideline is to keep the riding as light as possible, and to use the minimum amount of aids to achieve the maximum effect. There is something so negative about putting pressure on a horse with your riding and grinding him into submission and it can really put a horse off being ridden. You must, therefore, always looks for ways to make the aid language as light and pleasant as possible for the horse. The more you can ride from your seat aids and light hand aids the happier the horse becomes.

Canter to walk is a more advanced transition than walk to canter because more engagement of the hind leg is required and if the three joints in the hind leg are not suppled sufficiently they will stiffen against the demands of this transition; the horse will fall onto his forehand and come heavy into the hand. This transition is, therefore, best started when the rider has commenced collected canter. The best way to ride it is to half-halt the canter for a handful of strides, and then let your weight come down into your seat in order to sit heavily. Imagine your seat to be a flagstone, sit heavy for one stride, 'close' the seat for that moment for the last stride and then lighten again. It is the sequence of sitting heavily, closing and lightening that gives the effect. Do not sit heavy and just deaden the seat but ride with a positive, live deep seat, close the movement through the hips and then lighten to a live seat again for the last stride; the feeling of the extra weight will slow the horse into the downward transition. Initially, the horse can be allowed to make this transition progressively, i.e. coming down from canter to a *few* steps of trot and then to walk, and this is the easiest way to ride the transition at first. He will soon realize that you want canter to walk as you reduce the number of trot strides from four to five, then three to two, then down to one and finally you will have the full direct transition.

When running free, the horse can easily drop from a canter to walk, but when ridden he has to carry and balance the weight of the rider, balance himself and understand the aids that ask him to perform this transition. As stated, ride this transition progressively at first, make sure the horse is happy with all the other direct transitions and than quietly introduce canter to walk. Choose a place in the ménage that encourages the horse to come downward; as you approach a corner for example, and avoid places that may enliven him, such as coming out the corner towards the long side of the arena. Gather the canter up before the transition by sitting deeper, applying your legs, and just at the top of the canter squeeze on both reins while keeping the seat and legs still, and for the last stride sit with a heavy seat as a final indication to the horse that you want walk.

The simple change of lead is seen at the beginning of Elementary level. The horse changes canter lead by cantering forward and stepping into a few steps of walk before moving upward into the opposite lead. It gives the rider time to rebalance the horse, change bend and change aids. This type of simple change is easy and the horse may perform them well but when he reaches the stage of preparatory exercises for the flying changes and collection, he might start to evade the forwardness by giving you a backward feeling in your seat in the normal canter-to-trot and trot-to-canter transitions. This is because he has learnt the canter-to-walk transition, thinks he is clever and starts to anticipate. But this is not a situation where you should encourage anticipation and so you must calmly persevere with teaching the trot-to-canter transitions, the simple change of canter leads and canter-to-walk and walk-to-canter transitions alongside each other. Working through these different transitions keeps the horse obedient, listening to your aids, and helps the throughness of the forwardness.

He will soon progress through this blip, it is quite a normal blip so try not to worry about it, but do sandwich the simple-changes work with forward-going trot-to-canter transitions, and working to medium trot, i.e. powerful forward-moving gaits and tempos, and you will find both gaits improve as will the simple changes and the trot-to-canter transitions.

The reason we see both the simple changes and the trot-to-canter transitions in Elementary competition is to show the judge that the horse is *stepping through his back* in the transitions, and the simple change exercise has not been taught as a trick. Dressage is done to improve the beauty of the horse; the exercises help this and should never be performed as robotic movements. Dressage is horse gymnastics yet it transcends the physical plane into the realm of art. I believe this applies to the Novice just as much as the Grand Prix horse because a good and understanding relationship between horse and rider can develop this art at any level.

TIPS ON RIDING TRANSITIONS

To focus on the energy flowing forward, **ride with a live seat**. Advance in a sensible way, keep going, and do not beat yourself up every time you make a mistake. When you make a mistake say, 'OK, I've made a mistake, I'm going to correct it now, and start again.' Make it that simple.

Sit balanced by checking your position lines, i.e. shoulder–hip–heel and elbow–wrist–hand–bit lines, holding the rein according to the contact you have decided on – this is normally a contact rein (see Chapter 5) – squeezing with the lower leg, and allowing your seat to follow the movement as the horse moves forwards. Depending on the power of your horse this could mean you need to brace your back slightly, this feeling coming through your hips as if you were pushing a swing forward. This gentle bracing of the back absorbs the upward thrust of the horse's upward movement. This tends to happen more in downward transitions, and is the rider's way of handling the alterations in the horse's centre of gravity, which changes as you move from one gear to another. The bracing can be light, and taken through the stomach and hip muscles, or if riding a young powerful warmblood, and to ensure his back muscles are not restricted, the rider may put more weight onto the knee rolls through the thigh and knee, while keeping the upright upper body position of the modern dressage seat. This adaptation of the dressage position is often seen when training lively youngsters with big-moving gaits. We see many of the top riders adopting this position when riding young horses, even for certain movements of the canter if a horse has a sensitive back. Some horses are able to take the classical position and thrive on it. Others need an adapted riding approach that crosses classical with modern riding.

You must, therefore, **select the riding seat that helps the individual horse**. If you use the classical seat keep your seat light and do not push with it or you will flatten the horse's back, and the horse will not be able to round up through his back into the transition or allow the energy through from behind. If you use the modern seat, put a little weight into the knee rolls through the thighs and knees, lighten the seat, but stay sitting upright, otherwise you may drop the horse onto his forehand. The exception to this rule is that adopting a show-jumping forward seat with some young horses will help them flow forward more easily in the canter and their downward transitions are best ridden with this seat. However, keep the upward transition classical, sit up, and apply the classical aids precisely. (See Chapter 2, The Rider's Seat)

Sometimes powerful dressage horses, who often have show-jumping breeding lines, are so powerful in the hindquarters they are afraid of their power, perhaps because they are afraid of knocking themselves with their legs owing to this natural exuberance, and such powerful horses take little steps in canter to back away from the power that nature has given them. I listen to the hind hooves, and aim to hear a strong 1-2 beat, like the 1-2 beat a good show jumper performs just before takeoff, and I build up from this strength until the horse gains confidence, and by riding with a light, out-of-the-saddle seat the horse starts to round up through his back, and the canter grows stronger. By building up this strength and confidence, the horse takes bigger canter strides and soon he is moving in working canter. At this point the normal dressage position can be adopted, but perhaps still with a lighter seat.

The opposite can also happen with these powerful horses when they tend to overtrack forging forwards too much and driving themselves too much over the centre of gravity, and the same approach of looking for that strong 1-2 beat with the hind hooves, and sitting light, helps to build confidence and strength.

As stated, **big powerful horses can be frightened of their power**. They know they have this power but the restricted space of the dressage arena and carrying the weight of the rider suppresses their effusiveness and sometimes this turns into fearfulness. For example, they might be frightened of slipping on the arena surface. Such factors increase their nervousness, their back muscles tighten, and their balance depreciates. It is better to use a light non-pushy seat, to allow time for the horse to settle into his power and to understand canter is easy in a dressage arena. These horses often benefit from being cantered in straight lines out on a hack.

Keep the aligned shoulder-hip-heel position (the vertical alignment) and avoid clenching your buttocks or pushing into the horse's back with your seat. Imagine you have tiny eggs under the saddle, and if you sit too heavily you are going to break those eggs. That is how lightly you need to sit, and you should only utilize a more positive seat when your horse is well established and then only for short bursts of time. Always remember that your horse has muscles under the saddle, and nothing energizes them like transitions. Sit in a relaxed and comfortable manner in the vertical alignment, although in upward canter transitions I find it helps the rider to sit slightly behind the vertical for a few strides – because many riders find it difficult to resist being thrown slightly forwards in front of the vertical as the horse steps into canter – and then return to sitting on the vertical once the canter gait has been established. Only sit forwards if you have elected to do this for the specific reason of adopting the slightly forward show-jumping position.

Keep the contact the same. Normally, transitions are ridden on a contact rein, but whatever contact is decided upon it should remain constant, otherwise you are just chucking the rein at the horse at the moment of the transition and the horse will never learn to come through to the bit. The only exception to this rule is if a horse evades the transition as a resistance to a rider's aids; some young horses are inclined to do this. To overcome this resistance you can ease your elbows forward slightly towards the horse's ears by about a ¼–½ in (1 cm) to 'open the door' a little in order to allow the horse to come forward easily. Once he understands the requirement and responds appropriately, revert to the consistent contact rein, otherwise you are encouraging him to back away from the bit.

This tendency is often brought about by riders giving the rein unwittingly at the moment a transition is made: some believing they are riding with a light rein, some unconsciously pushing their hands down the horse's neck as if they are riding the horse over a jump, and others have the reins pulled through their fingers by the horse because their fingers do not have the correct feel around the reins. To overcome these faults check the length of the reins by putting markers on both reins, and check your hands remain in the same position, ideally no more than a few inches in front of the withers. If you make a mistake with the contact, correct it by closing your fingers around the reins as though squeezing a sponge lightly and apply your leg to nudge the horse forward into the contact. He will soon get the message; most horses are happy to comply and are much happier to go forward on a contact rein.

Throwing the reins at the horse at the moment of transition is common as is mistaking this action for the horse being light on the rein. Try to avoid this happening; it is preferable that a horse takes a bold contact than nothing at all – the horse being off the rein should never be mistaken for lightness. Throughness to the rein is so much a part of successful dressage that without it no true dressage is possible. Be aware of this but never punish yourself for mistakes, simply correct them as you go along, just keep going and you will be surprised at the results. Without throughness to the rein the horse is never taught to bend the hind legs, thereby strengthening the muscles, tissue and sinews, which in turn prepares him for collection and extension, elevation and better expression.

Use the lightest aid possible to get a forward response. Some horses go forward with the lightest touch of the calf muscles; some need more pressure on the stirrups. The lighter this pressure the more it is focused towards the toes putting the weight on the stirrups in a more precise way. Some horses require a firmer squeeze with the leg while others benefit from a light tap with the heel (although this is unusual). Keep your aids light, consistent and always apply them in the same way so that the horse identifies them easily. Always use the lightest aid possible to get a result. Remember that each horse has a different response time: Thoroughbred types tend to be quick off the mark and warmbloods tend to need a few seconds to listen; but, whatever your horse's particular response time, you must give him time to respond. Test this response period by counting it a few times. Although most riders find the transition happens automatically after the response time, you will not know if this is the case if you keep using your legs to get the response. This indicates that you are not being patient enough to wait for the horse's response time. Remember, your aids have to travel to the animal's brain and from his brain to his limbs and there is a transitory period while the horse's body reacts to the nerve impulses given.

Once you know your horse's response time (and it may differ for each transition. i.e. the walk to trot transition time could be different from that of trot to canter etc.) it becomes programmed into your riding seat and brain. As you learn to apply the aids to suit each individual horse, you will build up a library of response feel identifications by riding different horses and you will recognize that similar types react in the same way. These reactions are not dictated by breed or type of conformation but by similar reaction ratios.

Do not nag the horse. If you ask for a transition and demand an instant result when you are riding a slow-reacting horse, you may be tempted to nag him and pummel him with your legs, whereas if you are patient and wait for the reaction the horse responds well. It is not a sin to be a slow reactor; it is a sin to bully the horse. The temptation to do this is sometimes overwhelming, but *you must be patient*, and be precise and definite with your leg aids; you will then find that the reactions will improve. Responsiveness to the aids *does* improve with training, but the temperament and breed of the horse still affects it.

Assuming the horse has responded well to transition aids and begins a good transition, follow the movement with your seat but be careful not to block the forward momentum. If he has not responded (and you are sure you have allowed for his response time, as explained above), apply a firmer leg aid. If there is still no reaction, give a light tap with your stick to reinforce the leg aid. Never use the leg, or whip, aids in a punishing way, and *never* hit the horse with a schooling whip. Schooling whips were once termed 'cutting whips' and when used strongly can cut the horse's skin. **Remember**: this correct use of the whip is true of all good riding, not just dressage. The whip is a back-up to the leg aids, and never a means of punishment. This is important because, besides the humanitarian aspect, if you beat a horse his muscles will tense when he anticipates the whip touching him, resulting in a lack of trust leading to insularity and fear of his rider. In extreme cases these reactions can result in physical breakdown because the tension can cause muscle to tear. So always be compassionate and caring, never quick to punish or over-demanding. Everybody can get annoyed sometimes and if this happens dismount and put the horse back in his stable, or go for a nice quiet hack.

If your horse is light to ride, a light squeeze with the lower leg or just stepping more heavily on the stirrups is enough to ask him forwards to a transition. With this quick-reacting type be careful not to overdo the leg aids, because he will either jump into the transition or go too strongly into the rein, or become turned off by the aids. If you have sensitive hearing, for example, and somebody keeps shouting down your ear, it is a constant irritation. Similarly a sensitive horse will become irritated, get wound up or become resistant, or take to running off. Always be aware of your horse's needs, and his character, and ride accordingly. This way you will avoid having to correct counter effects, which hide real problems and take more skill to identify. For example, if a sensitive horse becomes wound up because of incorrect application of the aids he may get tense on the bit and you may view this, and try to correct it, as a contact fault, whereas the root of the problem lies in his sensitive reaction. In this instance, incorrect contact was the counter effect hiding the real problem of a sensitive horse dealing with the poor application of the aids.

Transitions reveal these situations, potential problems, and idiosyncrasies of each horse, better than most dressage exercises.

Riding upward transitions with some young horses is different from those ridden with trained horses because the young horse is not trained onto the aids as precisely as the trained horse. You do, therefore, need to think through each application of the aids and the horse's response to them in order to be able to know whether or not communication has been clear. You must avoid any fuzzy communication with a horse. For example, I use my leg in an on-and-off way with a young horse to make it completely clear that I require forward movement from the leg, but it can depend on the individual horse and his conformation. A comfortable horse that feels like an armchair is easy to sit to.

A round-barrelled horse is comfortable because your legs sit nicely around his body. However, if his ribs fall away by the shoulder, your lower leg can drop away from his sides too (especially if you are tall and the horse small) making it more difficult to apply the aids by squeezing with the lower leg. With these horses be flexible, it is better to sit in the classical position and apply the leg in an on-off, tap-tap way to help them understand the forward leg aid more easily.

Whatever the shape of the horse I like to have some part of my leg cuddling him at all times. This may be the leg just above my boot, or it may be my whole calf muscle. It depends on the way the horse is ribbed up and the way he likes to be ridden. I prefer a still seat, a comfy line from hip to knee and a relaxed lower leg, and this suits most horses. But no matter the shape, size, or type of the horse, I want him to be relaxed when I apply my leg aids, and this rule continues to apply when the aids are given in different places on his body and in different intensities.

If a horse is inclined to be lazy I will use a nudge-nudge leg, i.e. a leg that nudges, releases the nudge, and reapplies another nudge, but I am careful not to overdo the nudges, otherwise this can decline into a drummer-boy effect when the horse's sides are continually being banged by the rider's leg. This will cause the horse to switch off and become dead to the leg; you cannot blame him really, nobody likes to be nagged.

A sensitive horse may need the leg to cuddle him more firmly to gain confidence. If he becomes slow to my leg I am happy, because this tells me he has become confident; once I feel this I can sharpen him up to the leg, and he will move forwards to lighter aids. A fresh horse differs from a sensitive horse in that a fresh horse can sometimes demonstrate ignorance. When you put your leg on he will either shoot off or ignore it because he is too busy looking around and spooking. But, generally, a fresh horse benefits from having a relaxed leg on all the time, and if he ignores the leg, a nudge-nudge aid reminds him to listen.

Test a horse's response to the leg by going through transitions using the leg in the following sequence: a light leg aid, a reinforced leg aid, a tap with the whip to back up the leg aid; if there is still no reaction, apply a prick with the spur. You then return to the light leg aid for the next transition and always use the light leg aid for each transition initially, never using a stronger aid unless the horse is unresponsive. This gives a lazy horse the opportunity to come onto the leg aids in a quicker reactive way.

Using the whip as an artificial aid. I always prefer to use a short whip on the shoulder with young horses because they seem to respond better to a flick on the shoulder, whereas a tap behind the girth can frighten some horses. But a lazy horse may be happy to respond only to the whip and so I try to wean him off the whip by perhaps only using it during some training sessions.

I change to the schooling whip when I have used it for some time in work from the ground, or during lunge work. I really want to be sure the horse is not frightened of the whip, and if I think he is I do not carry one but quietly get him used to the riding aids without the use of artificial aids. Most horses will allow you to use a whip as an artificial aid if you use it kindly, but occasionally a horse will refuse to tolerate a whip. Do not worry; the simple answer is not to carry a whip. A horse like this might be doing you a favour because you cannot carry a whip in some qualifying championships, championships and the dressage phase of eventing competitions.

The voice can be helpful, especially when training transitions: an upward trill of the voice in a 'brrr' sound is good for upward transitions, and a downward 'brrr' is good for downward transitions. If you combine these voice aids with the leg aids the horse picks up quickly on what you want. If you use words, try using *walk on, trot on, gallop*, for upward transitions, and *walking, trotting*, and *ho-ho* for canter for downward transitions. There is more of an upward swing to the word 'gallop' that inflects the voice upwards and encourages forwardness, and 'ho-ho' calming and lower in tone to a horse's ears. 'Ho-ho' is a verbal aid used by carriage drivers and seems to work well for some strange reason. 'Whoa' sounds like 'walk' and can confuse the horse. Voice aids are especially useful when training young horses but should otherwise be used with discretion as they are not allowed in competition. Verbal aids are really a language specific to you and a horse and once his training is established they are dispensed with as riding aids, but kept to praise the horse. You can say whatever you like really but if it is said in a sing-songy voice, he will recognize he is being praised and horses love that! I often give a pat too but not too often if the horse is moving, because I want to keep a consistent contact on the reins. I will rub his neck gently to ease the inside rein because this helps self-carriage, but I am discreet about these movements of the hand to ensure I keep that steady feel on the rein.

Study your horse, take your findings into consideration and use the path that best helps your horse. Be flexible and educated in your training approach. I find that the most simple and easy way, the most compassionate and technically correct path proves to be the answer. Never try to force anything on a horse, always be compassionate.

HALF-HALTS

Riding a horse who moves in self-carriage is pure joy: he begins to lift off the forehand, bends the three joints of the hind legs and works in an elevated way of going that better expresses his gaits.

By riding different aspects of the half-halt individually, we begin teaching half-halts long before they are started properly. But when elevation starts to occur we have finer control, like driving a car with power steering, and the half-halt process is easier, and more enjoyable. To ride half-halts you have to feel the moment when to apply them. As stated, start conditioning the horse early on in his training through good transition riding and also by separating each dimension of the half-halt riding and teaching it step-by-step through the transition riding, because it is reflected in this work. If you have prepared your horse well through this work he will slip into the half-halts easily. Books explain that the half-halt is a simultaneous aid of seat, legs, and hands, to bring the horse to attention and balance. The Oxford Pocket Dictionary defines 'simultaneous' as 'occurring at the same time', but this proves that language is lacking when trying to explain the combination of feels needed to ride such a sensitive movement. Riding half-halts requires lightness from the horse in responding to the aids and sensitive application of them by the rider. Applying seat, legs, and hands at the same moment is unusual; more usually the seat is applied first, the legs a split second later, and then the hands are closed gently. The seat and legs can be used with a definite moment of separation, one before the other, or almost together and then held at the same degree of application while the hands are closed.

This sequence of seat and legs almost together, held constant, followed by the closed hands is especially suited to riding the canter. The hand aid is used when you feel the movement coming to the top of the canter and feel this movement as the energy comes up through the front of the saddle. It is not complicated if you ride transition work without using the hands to stop the forward momentum; remember that the hands are for flexion and direction only until the horse is really going forward to the bridle. Once this forwardness is achieved, a light softening on the outside rein will indicate to the horse that a transition is about to occur, and then the seat, legs, and both hands closing finalizes it.

The next stage of this half-halt work is to ride more positively into more direct transitions, e.g. trot to halt, and to ride them dramatically forward asking positively for willing responses from the horse. Some trainers say, 'drive in, drive out,' meaning drive your horse forwards into the downwards transition, drive him forwards into the upwards transitions. This requires positive leg aids, definite bracing of the back, and closing of the hands, and will bring about bending of the hind legs, rounding of the back into an active halt from trot, and a springing forward trot from halt. It is better to keep these half-halts on the straight, for example at E or B down the long sides, because the horse is moving along a straight line, the rider applies the aids equally with both sides of her body, and there is less room for error along the straight lines.

Joining half-halts to active, forward, progressive transition work. Check that the horse responds well to the aids, remains consistently forward, and is up to the bit. I check this self-carriage by quietly removing my lower legs from the horse's sides; if he continues moving forwards at the same rhythm and balance I am happy the training is progressing. To check the horse is not leaning on my hands to prop himself up I move my elbows towards his mouth by about a foot so that the contact is completely loosened. I do this for a handful of strides in trot and canter, and if he remains on the bit, i.e. in the same frame, without looking for the bit, or without coming above the bit, or altering his frame in any way, I know he is working towards self-carriage. These self-carriage conditioning exercises I add into the work early on, even during simple transition work, but I will increase them during the half-halt work to ensure: 1) that I am not over-riding the half halts, and 2) that the horse is responding easily and willingly.

By **trusting the horse** to react well to your aids, and to remain on the aids, without having to constantly reapply them in these self-carriage exercises, using the conditioning half-halt exercises as explained above, for example, always sorts out fuzzy areas of misunderstanding. In fact, I will add these exercises into half-halts in increments; for example, the allowing with the hand is done in tiny parts of an inch when I am taking a horse from Novice to Elementary levels and looking for more obedience stemming from the willingness of the horse to hold his own balance through self-carriage. If you read the collective marks on competition score sheets (e.g. from Preliminary to Medium levels) you will begin to realize the increasing importance of self-carriage, a willingness to respond to the aids, and impulsion, and these aspects are reflected in the half-halt and the transitions.

When a test asks for transitions sandwiched by a few strides of walk (e.g. trot to 3–4 steps of walk and to trot again) the rider is performing the start of half-halt work. The competition is priming her to think about half-halts without her realizing it. Thinking half-halts in this way is a healthy progression. In more advanced dressage, half-halts cannot be judged because they are mirrored through the work by the degree of balance the horse is showing. We see the joy of the horse working in self-carriage when we watch top competitors riding with apparently no effort, and seemingly giving no aids. It is as if the horse performs everything without direction; this invisible thread of communication coming from understanding training and good balance, a large proportion of which is gained from transition and half-halt work.

MORE GAIT TRAINING

It is important to understand the fundamental importance of focusing on the gaits and that transition work ridden forwards improves them dramatically. Once the basics of the working gaits are becoming embedded, improve the quality of the horse's way of going by turning your training thoughts to the different 'gears' in the gaits.

Developing the different tempos

'Tempo' describes the measure of speed within each gait. Rhythm should remain constant in each gait's tempo. For example, in collection the horse's legs will be raised higher than in extension but the rhythm remains the same. The table below summarizes general facts and information for easy reference, and the following text goes into more detail.

GAIT TEMPOS

THE WALK

Free walk   The horse is given a loose rein so that he can stretch his head and neck out and down free of any restrictions from the reins. He should march actively forward and show free-moving steps that express the maximum length of his steps when overtracking* without losing the four-time rhythm of the walk.

Medium walk   This is the natural walk of the horse but it is ridden with a touch more energy; the horse should overtrack and be on the bit. In the basic training the rider uses two types of walk: the free and medium walk.

Collected walk   In collection, the walk steps have more elevation than in medium walk and do not overtrack but track up. However, if a horse has a long back and tracks up in medium walk rather than overtracking (this is unusual), he will undertrack by the length of a hoof print in his collected walk. *Be very careful with this*, it is better to introduce a long-backed horse to collected walk when he is much more advanced in his training than a horse who overtracks in medium walk. The horse is in self-carriage with his neck raised and arched. Many trainers advise against teaching the collected walk any earlier than the second year of training.

---

*Overtracking is when the horse **steps over** the prints made by the front hooves with his hind feet and tracking up is when he **steps into** them.

Extended Walk   The horse is allowed to stretch his head and neck forward until the topline of the neck is approximately parallel with the ground, but contact with the horse's mouth must be retained. The walk strides cover as much ground as possible, i.e. they overtrack to maximum capacity without rushing and the regularity of the walk is in the four-beat rhythm.

THE TROT

Working trot   This tempo nearly matches that of the horse's natural trot except that a touch more briskness forwards is asked for. Most horses overtrack in the working gaits, but some track up (see above), and this depends on the way the horse moves naturally and on his conformation. For example, if the horse has a long back he is more likely to work in an active working trot but be tracking up and not overtracking. The main criterion is that the working trot is swinging through in active, rhythmical steps and the horse remains in balance.

Medium trot   This is developed through the working trot by encouraging the horse to take longer, more swinging through steps in the working trot. The horse moves with free strides which cover more ground than in the working tempo, and often keeps his balance by carrying his neck less arched than in the working trot and with his head slightly more in front of the vertical.

Collected trot   A horse is taught this trot after the basic training has been established; normally a year after training has begun. The steps are higher, the strides are rounder (moving in a forward-and-up way), the hindquarters are engaged, and the neck and head carried arched in a higher outline than in working trot.

Begin collected-trot work through riding the half-halts in the working trot, and be careful that after each half-halt the horse is urged forwards again with the seat and leg aids to refresh the forward momentum.

Extended trot   The rhythm of the trot is kept intact with the horse covering as much ground as possible and lengthening his steps to his maximum ability. This power comes from his hindquarters rather than the flicking of his toes forwards.

THE CANTER

Working canter   The tempo of this gait, like the working trot, nearly matches the horse's natural canter but a touch more energy is asked for. It is sandwiched between the medium and collected canter. Normally, it is taught when the horse is established in the basics and accepts the rider's aids in trot. Often the best way to develop this canter is by frequent transitions on the circle between trot to canter.

Collected canter   The hallmark of the collected canter is the lightness of the horse's forehand and engagement of his hindquarters so that his shoulders become mobile and his quarters active. A useful exercise for this work is 'stroking the horse's neck' to encourage self-carriage. This involves the rider moving both hands forward so that they are positioned, for a moment, several inches above the horse's mane and halfway along his neck; the rider then returns the hands to the original position, re-establishing contact with the horse's mouth.

Medium canter   With this canter the strides cover more ground, jumping forwards more in energetic steps that preserve the rhythm of the three-time beat. The horse remains in the same outline but normally carries his head slightly more in front of the vertical than in the other canter tempos.

Extended canter   When the horse extends he covers as much ground as possible while preserving the canter rhythm, and he lengthens his steps to the maximum of his ability through greater impulsion from his hindquarters. He remains on the bit, but normally lowers and extends his neck, his head being slightly in front of the vertical.

COLLECTION

Collection contains the horse's energy and gives elevation. It is a wonderful wheel of energy felt in the rider's seat. When the first stages of straightness begin to ripen, the training programme should be reassessed. The horse is approaching the cusp of true collection; he is on the verge of becoming a dressage horse. He will present a defined picture, his gaits become more beautiful, a crisper outline strikes the eye; an observer will want to see more of the picture.

You will feel the horse more willing to respond to the aids and excitement wells in the bottom of your stomach; you know this is what dressage is all about. The marriage between movement and the nature of the horse joined by the direction of the rider is about to happen.

Some riders, however, hear the word 'collection' and panic; others get despondent and back-off trying to ride collection. There is nothing to worry about; the only way is to move forwards: remember 'resting is rusting' the old masters say. It is better to be brave and advance.

Collection is about moving forward; everything in dressage is about forward movement, but it should be achieved in a progressive, not a sudden, way. Collection is easy when the rider approaches it one day at a time; it does not happen in a day, or on a specific day and the rider cannot wake up one morning and say, 'Right, today we will achieve collection.' But, when it happens, it will just drop into her lap like a ripe apple.

In fact, collection starts the moment the rider starts a young horse in transition work because well-ridden transitions resemble half-halts, and they are the backbone of collection. When you view collection in this light you will see how easy it really is. The danger with riding collection is often physiological and/or psychological; many riders hear the word 'collection' and start to think backwards, the hands clutch the reins, and the front of the horse is pulled backwards towards the hindquarters rather than being ridden correctly forwards. When the rider accepts the forward concept all is easy. If a mistake is made, it is simply corrected and then things can progress.

Collection brings self-carriage and a wonderful lightness to the steps. Giving the rein to the horse in small degrees to help attain self-carriage uplifts the collection (this is covered in more detail in Chapter 5). Pulling backwards shortens the horse's neck, restricts his back, cramps the joints in his hind legs, and makes him tight on the bit. All these effects tend to displace his shoulders away from the alignment with his quarters and ruin the straightness, and this further blocks the energy flowing through. A pronounced downward spiral of quality begins, which allows the horse to become strong and resistant to the rider's hands. To solve these collection problems, *backward riding must be forgotten.*

Collection is energy in a rounder frame. Collection keeps the true spirit of dressage, i.e. forward movement. If mistakes are made collect your thoughts, refresh the collection by riding the horse forward in brisk working gaits, or use the extra oomph of the medium and extended tempos, returning to the collected gait when the horse rediscovers his 'vavavoom' and feels like a sports car again! He should always feel like this.

If any shortening, i.e. the energy coming back to the rider's hands, happens the vavavoom shuts down. This can indicate the horse is not ready for collection, particularly if collection work has just been started. If this happens, return to the working gaits for a little longer, while at the same time picking up the simple preparatory collection exercises, e.g. direct transitions, small amounts of 10 m circle work, and more precise figure riding. Soon you can test the water with dashes of collection work and if all goes well you know the horse is ready for full collection training.

Establishing the working gaits is the first step in training the gaits. Preparatory medium trot and canter will already have been started, but alongside this work refresh the collection by frequently returning to the working gaits, and ensure that the horse steps over his centre of gravity while working within them.

Some horses established in collection work need periods of refreshment in the working gaits during, for example, periods of 'let off' time. This could be that he has, for example, not yet reached the peak of fitness during semi-rest periods, or at blackberry-coat time, during the autumn when the blackberries are ripe for pulling. It is at this time that a horse's libido goes off the boil as his body is making preparations for the coming of winter. The wise trainer uses this time to consolidate the foundations of the training (and of course the working gaits play a big role here) rather than pushing forwards with proactive work. In other words, the trainer takes the pressure off the horse and takes the natural way by following the rhythm of the seasons.

As stated, collection develops from transitions and half-halts, which make a horse more responsive to the rider's aids. In the collected walk and trot the hind feet step into, or just behind, the prints made by the forefeet. In the collected canter each stride is more elevated, rounder and more through. How the horse tracks up naturally should be observed and this is then used as a guide to his collected gaits. As an approximate measure, if a horse's working trot overtracks, his collected trot should track up, but if the working trot tracks up, the collected trot should undertrack, normally by the length of a hoof print.

THE RIDER'S SEAT IN COLLECTION

Your seat must be alive to the horse's movement and energy, and your hips must go with the movement or contain the energy depending on the situation and what is required. The receptiveness goes with the rhythm of the gait the horse is moving in, and the very quality of this receptiveness seems to lift the energy through the back, over the withers, and allows it to travel along the neck to the mouth. It streamlines the energy in a mystical way.

If you think you are blocking the forward momentum, or your seat loses the lightness and receptiveness needed for riding collection, slip into rising trot, or canter position out the saddle, for a short burst of time. This more basic seat allows the horse to feel his back being freed, and you should soon be able to return to sitting more upright in collected trot, for example. It is important that you are sensitive to the effects of your seat on the horse's way of going in the collected tempo, and his reactions to the aids. Dressage training is not like playing Russian roulette, but a steady build up of a horse's strength and confidence, and a joining together of the horse's and rider's skills so that they understand each other better.

Ride with a light seat that allows the horse to work forward, *a lifting up of the rider's ribs and hips helps the lift in collection*, thus allowing the energy to flow through more easily, and a bracing of your back prompts the horse towards moments of increased power through transitions and half-halts. This lifting up of your upper body brings more lightness to the steps.

MEDIUM AND EXTENDED TEMPOS

As explained, once the basic working gaits are established, you then branch out into the different tempos. The order of work would be: medium trot and canter, collected trot, collected canter – putting a little extended work into all three gaits – and lastly collected walk. This is the normal order for developing the tempos because it avoids backward thinking and keeps the gaits active and forward especially in the collection. Of course there are exceptions, for example, if a horse is hot and has a natural spring in his steps that lends itself to collection without stifling the energy, but too much medium and extended work makes him nervous, then doing the collected work first will still help progression with balance and self-carriage. Also, if a horse lacks expression in the medium and extended tempo but works obediently forwards to expressive working gaits, the collection can be introduced first, alongside small amounts of medium and extended work. However, if you are inexperienced with collected work and are worried about undoing the working-tempo work, it would be wise to follow the prescribed training route. This way you will avoid disappointments and be sure you are training along the correct classical lines.

Exercises for starting medium trot

A good way to start the work on medium trot is simply to encourage bigger working trot strides (Figure 4.11). Gradually the horse will become eager to step out more. The feel he should give is that if you were to ask him for even more he would respond positively: if you could just open the door more the horse would step through, and with a whoosh forwards to bigger steps. It is an automatic progression. By building up the medium steps in this gradual way, it takes the pressure off horse and rider.

There are three exercises that will help the journey to medium trot.

1. Ask for a few strides of powerful forwardness in the trot and then temper it with working trot again by softening the seat to a working-tempo speed through sitting live with the seat to give direction to the horse to come

Figure 4.11   Working towards medium trot

forward and down to the working-trot tempo. If the horse's response is not smooth enough, you can soften with the hand as you feel the horse stepping from the few medium steps to working trot.

Once a horse has started to assimilate this work a little, if he flags after a few steps he can be half-halted to bring him onto his haunches, and then be allowed forward again to perform more medium strides. He will need to be established in half-halt work, and to be eager to respond to the forward aids, but these aids are often needed with horses developing the medium trot.

2.   Some horses like to be cranked up to medium trot. You ask for a more rounded, active trot in the corner, through the first corner of the short side of the arena in working trot, and ride out of the second corner in a powerful brisk trot. Once a horse gets the idea he will start to step into medium strides.

Start this training with just a few strides of medium trot and, once the horse understands what is required, consolidate this work before building up gradually to more strides. Eventually the horse will perform a full-throttle medium trot from marker to marker and/or as and when required.

3. Medium trot can be taught while hacking out if you select the right terrain. Find a long hill, start at the bottom in an active trot, and, as you go up the hill, gradually ask with the legs for more extension. Some horses like a rider to sit with the weight going into the saddle flaps through the knees, but without tipping forwards. This position frees the horse's back and allows the steps to flow forward. Once he has responded, ask for the same exercise at the same hill every time you ride it until the horse anticipates the exercise and goes into medium strides automatically. Begin this new exercise halfway up the hill but gradually it can be started at the bottom and continued to the top. He will get keener, anticipate more, believe he is being clever, and enjoy the work, but this anticipation must be positive and work in your favour, i.e. providing you always give clear aids to ask for medium trot, the anticipation can be allowed.

Once you reach the brow of the hill, ask the horse to return to walk, and walk him quietly down the other side. If any gait other than walk is used, it should be collected trot, because you want to avoid him slipping as he goes downhill.

Medium trot is required in Elementary-level dressage tests, but not at Preliminary or Novice levels.

Tips on riding medium trot
Most horses find it easier to do this preparatory work in rising trot, but some prefer sitting trot because they gain comfort from the rider's sitting-trot seat, and providing the seat is supple and allows the movement through it can be used instead of rising trot. These horses tend to be the exception rather than the rule. Avoid sitting behind the vertical, i.e. behind the shoulder–hip–heel alignment, if sitting trot is used; keep the seat alive with the movement and almost lifting a

little through the seat as the energy comes from behind and travels forward to the front of the saddle. Avoid blocking the energy from coming through.

Some horses like to move with a rounder outline than is classically prescribed, which is acceptable initially. To achieve this, soften the horse on the bridle in a rounder outline and ride the medium steps. You can accept a tiny bit of lifting of the poll providing the steps are elevated and free flowing but correct this fault slowly through transitions within the gait and half-halts and you will find the horse softens the poll and maintains the rounder outline. If, on the other hand, you insist on 100 per cent correctness from the beginning, the freedom of the steps can be lost easily. Round him through his back after the medium strides; gradually he thus learns to keep a round outline into, through, and out of, this tempo. Once he can maintain a steady outline, adopt a more classical approach where he moves in a less rounded outline and his head and neck are held more parallel to the ground than in the collected tempo.

On the contrary, other horses like room to stretch their head and necks parallel to the ground, which is not classically prescribed, but this too is acceptable initially. This must be allowed for by a softening of the elbows towards the mouth as the horse steps into the medium trot. He must not, however, be allowed to drop the contact as the elbows are softened and you must be careful not give too much rein otherwise the horse will drop off the bridle and onto the forehand.

To ride well in a way that trains constructively, you often have to experiment with different methods; however, the results quickly indicate which way to progress. You check the horse and he steps into the rein in this new tempo of medium trot. Some horses like you to take more feel on the rein for medium trot.

Some horses love medium trot so much that the rider can use it to reward them for doing a new exercise; it is like giving them a treat.

Extended trot

Extension requires more oomph than the medium strides; in fact, extension requires more of everything: more energy and more ground being covered, but the principles are the same. Medium trot will already have been established and a horse simply has to be asked for a little more forward energy, like a door being opened. This work is approached in the same way as the medium work. The extended trot is the ultimate expression of forward movement in the trot and has the highest degree of activity and swing through the horse's back. It is the climax of the gymnastic development of the horse with the longest period of suspension. It is the longest time the horse must carry the rider while all four legs are off the ground, and this takes lots of physical stamina. It is, therefore, easy to appreciate why extension comes from collection, and is developed over many years training.

You must begin with just a little extension and refine the straightening work, because this allows energy through, combining this with the collected work; once collection has been established, extension will slip into place.

Some horses are born with a top gear, a natural expression in their steps that automatically gives medium and extended strides. Sit in preparation for the movement so that your hips will absorb the extra power coming through the horse's back. Some horses find this top gear comes easily, others are not so endowed by Nature and each stride needs to be coaxed out of them, but you should not worry that the steps will not come with training because, providing the training is approached sensibly, all horses will be able to work in these tempos. The key is to find the best way to help each horse discover it is easy and this takes patience and steady training.

Medium and extended walk

The medium walk is the working tempo of the walk and the horse should be working on the bridle. He marches forward, overtracking, and accepts the bit with a soft contact. Horses have no difficulty with medium walk. You will be wise to use it for specific exercises such as teaching the lateral work, and to intersperse it with periods of walk on a long rein, or loose rein for most walk exercising.

Here is a comment from the top international dressage judge, David Trott taken from our co-authored Allen Photographic Guide, *Preparing for a Dressage Test*: 'The horse is asked to march forwards in front of the rider's seat, is *allowed to draw his head and neck down and forwards towards the ground with his nose slightly in front of the vertical and to move with his back and neck rounded. This allows maximum opportunity for relaxation and a chance to show overtracking of the footfalls without losing the four-time rhythm.'*

It is this freedom, this 'allowing', that lets the horse relax his back muscles so that the energy (that is restricted by lack of suspension) to step from behind through to the front (Figure 4.12).

ENCOURAGING FREE WALK ON A LONG REIN

1. Use free walk on a long rein frequently for short periods of time for relaxing rest periods sandwiched in between the schooling exercises. The horse has already worked actively forward in the trot and canter gaits and used his back muscles; he will want to stretch his head down more. The energy moves through and he has a natural need to step through (overtrack) more freely. If he resists this freedom, prompt him forwards with alternate use of the calf muscles against his sides. Leave each nudge for a longer period of time against the horse's sides if you want a longer stride forward.

2. Once the horse is happy with free walk on a long rein being used for relaxation, it can be used specifically as an exercise, simulating that which you will have to do in a dressage test, across the diagonal for example. The horse must be ridden in a more rounded outline in medium walk, turned on to the diagonal line and straightened; the reins can now be quietly eased by allowing them to slip through your fingers. When on the long rein, he is allowed to stretch his head and neck forward and down while you use encouraging nudges with alternate calf muscles to get him to step forward at the same time. If he remains reluctant to step forward properly you must make sure you are not blocking him with your seat by keeping it light but active, and indicating the forwardness required by your seat following the movement through the saddle from the cantle to the pommel. If your seat is tight you will block the overtracking but if you press the seat bones into the horse's back in a more positive way *while keeping the hips supple with the walk movement* you can help the overtracking of horses not as free as they should be in this work.

Figure 4.12   Walking on a loose rein, the horse stretches down during a rest period. There could be more stepping through from behind, but he is stretching down well and nicely through the topline.

MEDIUM CANTER

Establish straightness in the canter work before starting to teach medium canter. Ride into the corner in an active canter, position the horse's shoulders *very slightly in front* of his hindquarters by taking a *very slight* shoulder-in position, and then ride forward into the medium canter. Many horses love it if you sit slightly behind the vertical and anchor your seat firmly in the saddle but when you want to bring the horse forwards to a rounder canter, sit vertically and lighten the seat. Most horses respond to these different seat positions easily because they follow the centre of gravity of the rider's position. The also love to gallop! It follows, therefore, that they will love a big onward-going canter, it is in their nature.

If a horse is a little too keen you must contain the forward energy by holding the horse with your seat as you would with a downward transition to collection.

Lift up through the ribcage to lift the movement upwards and soften your contact on the outside rein with gentle give-and-take movements; this will remind him to come into a more controlled tempo but to keep a springy step, and move into a round outline.

EXTENDED CANTER

Avoid doing too much extended canter until the horse is working well at Medium Advanced level, asking for only a little extended canter in the same way that only a little medium trot should be ridden at Novice level. Riding a good extended canter requires high levels of straightness and stamina from the horse and overdoing it can cause strains.

Medium and extended tempos can be ridden on open areas of grass where there are long straight lines to cover, but do be careful. It is so easy for a horse to slip on grass, and so make sure he is wearing studs. You must also know the lie of the terrain and be sure that there are no rabbit holes, deep patches or other possible dangers.

Good training guarantees quality gaits. If the training is tackled in a logical, thorough and dedicated manner, the results will be excellent. When a horse swings through his back into an elastic contact, the gaits become regular and the energy flows through in a steady stream of power.

Figure Riding

Dressage has been designed to be ridden in an arena laid out with set markers at prescribed points to allow the accuracy of the work to be measured. When a young horse starts his training, strict accuracy may not be insisted upon, but as the schooling progresses the riding of correct figure work increases in importance.

CORNERS

When riding a young horse, initially the corner can be approached by either going round it in a large smooth arc, allowing him plenty of space, which is the classical method, or by riding through it in walk in a square shape, which is the more modern method. With the latter, you should maintain a slight outside bend on the approach to the corner, straightening him just before the apex, and then bending him slightly to the inside as he is ridden out; although it is useful sometimes to show a horse what a corner is by simply halting him in the corner and giving him a pat before riding the corner as two straight lines. Once the horse can perform this two-straight-lines approach to a corner in walk it can be done in trot but riding a corner in canter with this approach is best left until the horse is working well in collected canter.

In reality, most riders combine both of the above methods because the two-straight-lines approach helps the corners to be performed with a degree of precision beyond the horse's level of training. For example, if a horse becomes unbalanced going round a corner he will cut off the corner more, or altogether, and negotiate it like a motorbike going fast round a tight corner so that it resembles part of a curve of a 20 m circle. Obviously this does not help training! This modern method does, however, have the disadvantage of not encouraging straightness or the bending of the hind legs, which is fundamental to circle work, and riding the curve of the corner correctly is the basis of good circle riding. Remember the maxim that every corner is an opportunity to produce a beautifully moving horse and learn to treat each corner as an indispensable tool to success in your dressage work. The better you ride corners, the better your dressage will be.

When a horse has reached Novice standard, you may warm him up by riding in rising trot. Give him *plenty of room around corners* if he needs to be pushed on to get the blood flowing through his body, or if he tends to be lazy, or takes short strides, not stepping over the line of his centre of gravity, but after ten minutes of riding him around the arena and giving him plenty of room around the corners you start correct corner-riding work, i.e. riding into the corners in an active way of going and not cutting the corners off.

When riding a test you will always show the difference between each corner as you approach the start of a circle, for example a 20 m circle at A. Ride into the first corner, finish and start the circle at the same point, and then, with this example, ride into the second corner before the long side of the arena. It is attention to such details that not only add to the prowess of the horse but also marks the competent rider out from the crowd. This rider will know that such careful riding will earn extra marks, and that the whole arena can be used giving the horse more freedom to move better.

Sometimes the horse may need exercising in a space that is larger than an arena, and this is acceptable for very large circles in canter, for example, but generally the dressage horse is always trained in a measured dressage arena of 20 m by 40 m or 20 m by 60 m.

GOING LARGE AND STRAIGHT-LINE WORK

Going large is riding around the perimeter or outside track of an arena, without circling.

Straight-line work can be ridden along the long and short sides of the arena, the half, quarter and three-quarter lines and any lines cutting straight or diagonally across the arena. For example, once a horse has completed a circle and has come through the second corner, the front of the horse should be straightened before the relevant quarter marker (K, M, H, or F, which are always positioned 6 m away from the corner) and then ridden in a straight line towards the next corner. If the horse is young and not yet started his straight work he may wobble a little in his balance, but if he is ridden more forward, this straightens him up. Because he has not yet begun this work, initially he must be ridden with equal feel on both reins and no inside bend, and because he is narrower through his shoulders than his quarters, he will not strictly be moving straight along that straight line. You have to live with this shortfall until training progresses.

Bend complements straightness

Gradually, through the suppling of circles, correctly ridden corners and lateral shoulder-in work, the horse becomes straighter, and you can keep the outside contact while showing a small degree of inside bend. It may take some time to reach this point in training, but if you want to show extra spring to the horse's steps while he moves in trot along the long side, you can ask for inside bend *just for a few moments*. You can use this technique for showing the horse at his best for special occasions such as competitions and showing classes but generally it is best avoided because it is too tempting for the horse to hang on the inside rein and lose the outside contact, and it is the outside contact that gets inside bend.

When the horse is more experienced the rider *sits very slightly more to the inside*, and *positions the horse's poll to the inside very slightly*. This positioning is only about half to one inch and a maximum of two inches – a tiny amount – yet the rider sits towards the movement with the *inside hip very slightly forward* and the weight *very slightly more on the inside stirrup*. This positioning riding helps inside bend and increases straightness and suppleness; in fact, all figure work will do this if performed correctly.

CIRCLES

A horse is started on large circles, and in a dressage arena the maximum-sized circle is 20 m. But it may be some time before a young, or a stiff, horse is capable of holding his balance around a large circle without losing the energy through the shoulder, slipping the quarters out, or leaning on the rein, and because rhythm and contact come before straightness (and this requires accuracy on the circle as explained in the Straightness section on page 150), the horse is allowed to move on a slightly oval shape. You must focus on keeping the contact consistent, the outline steady, and the rhythm of the gait regular; you will find this comes first in trot and then canter. Gradually, over a period of time the horse will be able to negotiate a large circle and maintain balance so that rhythm, contact, spring, and straightness remain consistent. This work is always performed first in the working gaits. To achieve accuracy you can place bollards at four points around the circle and ride between them making sure the horse makes steps equal in size and number around each bollard while remaining in the same rhythm. The same principle is applied to 15 m circles.

Smaller circles can be started in walk at Preliminary level and are seen in competition in such movements as two 10 m half circles joined in the middle of the arena, and a half 10 m circle in trot returning to the track in the teardrop shape of a loop. Mark out in your mind's eye the placing of each half circle and allow the horse to step through it in a smooth flowing movement.

When a horse is ready for smaller full circles you must adopt a different riding technique. Practise by sectioning off a corner with poles to a shape of approximately 10 m square. Start by walking around the square, riding neatly into each corner, and while still in walk, describe a circle shape by cutting off each corner. Imagine you are snipping off the corner with a pair of scissors, touching the track, riding on it for a few strides, snipping off the next corner, and so on. Make sure your shoulders and hips stay parallel with those of the horse and, because he is moving on a smaller circle shape, you will have to position them accurately to the line of the shape to ensure you stay sitting square to axis. Once the horse is happy with this exercise you may ride round the outside of the square markers in a neat working trot, and then re-enter the square to do a 10 m circle in trot using the same corner-snipping technique.

Don't be concerned if the circle is not perfectly round, because this is impossible until collected work has begun, but as long as the flow of the trot is consistent, the contact remains good, and the line of the circle-type shape is maintained steadily you can be happy with the work. You will in fact be working on more of an octagonal shape (eight straight lines joined together). This is ironic because we see small circles in Novice-level dressage competitions, yet strictly, as already stated, they cannot be accurately ridden until collection starts. There is, however, no doubt that there are benefits in riding them if they are done intelligently.

You must be careful not to overdo riding small circles, or in fact over-riding any size circle, but be aware that you should be interspersing circle, and figure, work with riding on straight lines by going large around the arena.

Every time a horse moves through a circle it is an opportunity for the horse to come into better balance as explained. He automatically bends the three joints in his hind legs on a circle, and it elevates him off his forehand in preparation for collection; you will also soften/bend through the body better.

LOOPS AND SERPENTINES

These vary in depth and shape: some are shallow loops that run along the long side of the arena, some look like spaghetti loops and go across the arena from edge to edge, and some are like the curves of a circle joined with straight lines. At the lower competition levels the shapes tend to be easy such as a loop from one quarter market to the next, coming off the track to a maximum of 5 m with the widest point of the loop being at the half marker.

Start to ride this loop by keeping the existing inside bend you have and riding smoothly towards the point opposite the half marker that measures 5 m in from the track; just before that point, gently straighten the inside bend and then position the horse to the outside. Place your outside leg forward on the girth as if it were the inside leg, and put more pressure through your calf muscles to keep the horse from going back to the track too quickly. He will have a desire to go back to the track and try to lead with his outside shoulder, but by connecting the new outside rein (which was the inside rein) and by keeping a steady pressure with the leg maintaining the bend he should keep each side of the loop equal. Once the horse returns to the track at the furthest quarter marker the bend is changed again to inside bend. The bend sequence was: inside bend, outside bend, inside bend; riding the bends correctly proves beneficial and they supple the horse.

The same principle applies to every loop of the serpentine shape. You must always be aware of the bend that is needed, always reconnecting to the new outside rein, and applying the new inside leg and inside bend, keeping the flow of the gait coming through regularly. The size and length of the loop, or loops, must be maintained, as must the distance from, or to, the track.

TIPS ON FIGURE RIDING

You will do well to consider the geometry of dressage and acknowledge that figure riding automatically makes your horse go better. A good way to understand dressage figures is to watch riders performing them, and to pace them out on foot in an arena. For example, if a figure new to you is being asked for in a competition you have entered, think it through, measure it out proportionally according to the size of the arena, and then pace it out on foot placing accurate markers to act as focal points to help you ride the figure, and keep practising it. If you are smart you will have your home arena already marked out, either with bollards spaced for the figures you want to practise, or with paint markers around the edges.

The only way to truly get an eye for correct figure work is to repeatedly ride it accurately by following correctly spaced markers. Over a period of time you will automatically know if a horse is evading the movement, either through disobedience or stiffness, and by being able to instantly discern this incorrect work you can correct it immediately, which saves a lot of time and energy when training the dressage horse.

Perfecting figure riding is often neglected, but not only does it give super results in training it also gains loads of marks in dressage competitions.

The Straightening of the Horse

The Spanish Riding School has a saying that you would do well to remember: 'Train your horse forwards and straight.' Without straightness there can be no true energy coming through. Energy should travel equally through both sides of the horse to both sides of the bit to be effective. But, the horse is narrower through the forehand than the hindquarters and also has a tendency to cling to the edges of the dressage arena, and these two factors make him crooked. There are different ways to straighten the horse.

- Keep the head and neck of the horse straight in front of his withers so that the energy does not escape to left or right, and introduce bend gradually, again so that the energy does not escape. Avoid asking for too much inside bend. Avoid pushing the horse too far forward beyond his balance or allowing him to move without enough activity to maintain free flow forwards and keeping the hind legs following the shoulders.
- Correct riding of figures such as corners and circles.
- Suppling exercises to straighten the hollow side and soften the stiff side of the horse; for example, inside leg to outside rein exercises, the unilateral half-halt (see Chapters 5 and 6).
- Avoid pulling on the inside rein and ride the horse on both reins.
- Counter canter (for exercises see page 106).

A horse will be crooked until well trained. The degree of crookedness varies with each horse depending upon his conformation and if he is stiff on one side due to a lack of dressage training. Many horses move straight when trotted up in hand on straight lines and this will give you a clue to his ability to move straight naturally. But for dressage a more refined straightness is required, the horse has to move straight on straight lines and straight while moving on circles and curves. To be straight on circles and curves successfully he has to stretch the outside of his body more than the inside, this allows his hind legs to follow the prints of his front legs, and for his body to follow the line of the circle.

No horse is 100 per cent straight because his body does not allow it, just as no human being can be completely ambidextrous, but when the training progresses the degree of straightness will improve. The degree of straightness expected of a Novice and a Grand Prix horse is markedly different, and we see this in the movements required for these different levels. For example, the Novice horse is asked to show straightness on 20 m circles and in simple counter-canter exercises, the Grand Prix horse has to show straightness on 6 m circles and in counter-canter on tight loops. Viewed from this aspect, the relationship of straightness to collection can be appreciated.

Training straightness requires time, a gradual suppling of the horse's body from the tail to the nose. The generally accepted steps of training are:
1) Looseness (i.e. suppleness)
2) Rhythm
3) Contact
4) Throughness and spring
5) Straightness
6) Collection.

In theory the components of training are clear cut, but in practice they blend into each other. For example, you start with rhythm and contact and, as it develops, spring comes through. The straightening exercises are performed alongside this preliminary training work but once the basics are established they increase in dimension. Once straightness is established the energy flows through the horse's body smoothly, it is not wasted by being lost through either side of the bit, or the horse's quarters, or his shoulders. This increased straightness allows the energy to flow through an improved outline ready for collection work. In fact, without good straightness the collection will be mediocre, and to move towards better straightness start as above.

RIDING INSIDE LEG TO OUTSIDE REIN

Ultimately, you want to be able to ride the horse on both reins with an equal feel at all times, but this rarely happens to begin with. You can get close to it through riding exercises such as inside leg to outside rein and the unilateral half-halts (see Chapter 5). The former is the most accepted way to start straightening work besides figure riding.

Inside leg to outside rein means the horse is steady on the outside contact so that the inside contact can be softened. This softening can be a tiny degree, or a generous arm's length. The horse is connected to the outside rein by the inside leg, but you must be careful because if the energy is right you do not ask for more, but by sitting towards the movement, i.e. sitting square to axis for the line of the circle, you automatically weight your inside seat bone, and this acts as your leg. However, to start the movement many horses like an indication with the inside leg, a more elastic feeling on the outside rein, a slight positioning to the inside through the poll, and a softening on the inside rein. These aids are defined and given according to the needs of each horse. The outside contact takes priority, and the aids are applied separately but in a sequence that makes them seem like they are almost joined together. A young horse is normally taught inside leg to outside rein gradually, when changing the rein for example.

Exercises for teaching inside leg to outside rein

A simple exercise is to teach inside leg to outside rein in walk on the circle, followed by trot on the circle, and lastly canter. The circle makes it easier to connect up to the outside rein because it automatically increases engagement of the inside hind leg and thereby gives a better opportunity for the horse to accept a healthy contact on the outside rein. For these reasons it is the preferred figure to use when riding this exercise.

Position the horse slightly to the inside by approximately ½ –2 in (2–5 cm) keeping a steady elastic feel on the outside rein. Soften your leg more on the girth, and feel a connection up to the bit and a healthier acceptance of the outside rein. Some riders find it easier to practise this exercise in halt before progressing to walk. You can refine this exercise of slight positioning to the inside, or outside, while riding large in general work if the horse tightens on the rein or there is a lack of energy coming through (this is covered in greater detail in Chapter 5).

It is good to position to the outside and inside through corners, or when riding canter because a very slight positioning to the outside (almost like a feeling of positioning rather than actually positioning) helps you to check that your horse is up to the outside rein for the canter. You may have started the canter transition with inside bend (as is normal and classical) but you will then make a slight outside positioning of the poll to keep the horse straight in the canter.

The more advanced exercise is counter-canter, a very good straightening exercise for the canter. A horse has no difficulty with counter-canter but often it is the rider who must get to grips with riding true canter reversed. It is just logical thinking and boiling the counter-canter exercises down to make it simpler (see photographs 4.10a and b).

Straightness develops slowly and straightness is not just how the horse moves with his legs, but correct bend through the body. The greater the curve of a circle, the more bend through the body is needed, and the more suppleness shown through the horse's ribcage. A fundamental of dressage is: *move forward and straight with your horse, move forward and straight with your heart*. Just as the show jumper cannot win without throwing his heart over the jump, so the dressage rider cannot progress without throwing her heart towards straightness.

Balance

The way a horse moves expresses his balance, and the dressage rider's aim is to improve the balance so that the horse can move more freely while carrying the rider's weight. The moment you sit on a horse you upset his balance, but training brings him into better balance. The weight comes off the forehand and is distributed over the four legs more, and sometimes the balance expresses itself in elevation, lightness and self-carriage.

Normally, it takes six months to a year to establish the foundation of dressage balance in a horse. Once he progresses to collection he receives a boost in balance training and this improves his entire carriage and posture.

The basics are important; if you take the time to establish the basics, the horse gradually learns to come under your weight without losing balance. This balance training relates to gymnastic training because the horse cannot be suppled without it, nor can he be suppled correctly if he is unhappy and tense. Nothing worthwhile will be achieved without the cooperation of the horse, and so you must advance with the work a little bit at a time so that the basics act as a safety valve. If problems occur, always revert to the basics to re-establish the horse's balance; for example, if there is not enough bounce in the collected canter return to the working canter to refresh it. Going back to previous training stages will refresh the basics for a few minutes, a working session, weeks, or months, depending on the scale of the problem, and the horse's physical ability to adjust to correction. Well-bred horses tend to respond better because they have inherent traits of stamina and muscle tone in their physical make-up.

Each horse's balance is peculiar to him and it differs at each stage of his training. You will know if things have gone wrong if the horse: looks scrunched up, is too collected, falls on his forehand, swerves off track, swings his quarters away from the line he is travelling on, gets too heavy in the hand, or if there is not enough energy coming through and the contact lightens too much in relation to the energy coming through and his degree of training; these all indicate that the balance is wrong. Often the simple remedy is to ride a transition or half-halt, or a straightening exercise such as inside leg to outside rein.

Always check that there is *enough energy* flowing through the horse's body but that there is not *too much energy* or he will tip on his forehand, and not *too little energy* or he will feel stuffy and not flow forward freely. But balance relates to the level of training, it is a combination of the horse's posture, the suppling of his hind legs, the lifting of his forehand, and the gymnastic toning of his muscles. The hindquarters are the motor of the horse, the forehand is the steering, the back connects front to back and is the place the rider sits. The energy must travel through the horse's body while it carries the weight of the rider in the middle, and it is this constant stream of energy contained in a steady outline relative to the horse's way of going that gives balance.

You have to ride in harmony with the horse in order to get balance, and this means you have to sit well, and understand how to apply the aids, and when. You allow new exercises to grow from the basic training in a natural way that does not put undue stress and strain on the horse's psychological make-up, or on his physical wellbeing and the only real way to achieve this is by a steady build-up of exercises.

Establishing the basics well separates the well-trained horse from the untrained one, and will give a stamp of quality to his way of moving. Such a horse gives you a wonderfully relaxed 'aaah' deep-breath-in-and-out feeling, a feeling that no matter what happens you can handle the situation, because you have the basics to rely on. You have been responsible for training your horse within a partnership: your superior intelligence and the horse's superior body.

The riders of the Spanish Riding School say, 'The horse can do dressage without the rider but can he do dressage without the horse?' Having watched horses moving freely in fields, you want to emulate the beautiful 'dance' you see when you ride. You want to deepen that horse and rider relationship, but you must remember that even the smallest pony is stronger than a strong man, and that training relies on cooperation, understanding and technique – never on brute force.

CENTRE OF GRAVITY

Balance and centre of gravity are connected. The dressage horse's centre of gravity is positioned approximately in line with the girth. The first aim is to ride the horse forward in the working gaits so that his hind legs step over the imaginary line of his centre of gravity with each stride. The working gaits encourage this stepping over, and it explains why they play such an important part in establishing the fundamental training of the dressage horse.

Getting stuck in a rut with training can unbalance a horse. He has developed his balance and is ready to show collection, and if you insist on carrying on at one level when he is ready to move to another, this can unravel his balance. However, reverting to transition and half-halt work often overcomes every problem.

It is not possible to measure the line of the centre of gravity precisely because it alters according to the speed, the distribution of weight of the horse and rider, the horse's conformation, and the gait he is moving in. You can recognize dressage balance by comparing it with that of a racehorse or a show jumper. The racehorse gallops over the ground stretching his body to cover as much ground as possible with each stride (the energy moves horizontal to the ground), a show jumper moves his centre of gravity forwards when he jumps so that it is vertical to the ground. The dressage horse is balanced well on four legs, with the hind legs engaged and the energy moving neither vertically nor horizontally but upward and forward. It feels like the energy rises up in front of the pommel of the saddle as he lightens his forehand to express movement. The power is like driving a fast car with power steering, or Concorde taking off.

The subject of the centre of gravity confuses many people yet is simple when you study it. I thought it might be possible to identify the horse's centres of gravity by using a wind tunnel. My father had a deep understanding of this subject; he built aircraft and each type has its own centre of gravity. I wanted to use his expertise and make a model of a horse to see if measuring its centres of gravity in a wind tunnel would help explain the subject. But later I realized it would be impossible because horses are flesh and blood and their centres of gravities are alive and move within them.

The best way to understand different aspects of balance is to ride a horse and feel them. Riding a trained dressage horse can help you feel the different tempos. We have all experienced moments when a horse gathers himself up in natural collection to spook, to jump, to be naughty; he is like a cat ready to pounce.

When the horse moves upward and forward the weight lifts off his forehand and his front limbs are protected from wear and tear. He becomes noble looking, more beautiful with each step becoming bigger, cleaner, freer, enabling you to direct the energy more precisely; the free flow comes through, opening the door for better balance.

5 CONTACT

CONTACT IS A mysterious entity, the steady hand doing nothing yet working miracles. There are countless benefits for a rider with good hands, the effects are amazing. But what is contact? Different schools refer to it by different names: on the bit, in flexion, on the bridle, acceptance of the bridle, all are derived from the classical interpretation.

We see that lovely expression of energy when a horse is well on the contact, he moves upward and forward. If he stiffens, his poll must just be lowered a little and the leg applied to energize the horse upward and forward again. This classical outline represents the correct outline and came from training classically bred horses such as the Lipizzaner and Andalusian. However, today's sport horses differ in physiology and, consequently, different forms of teaching softness to the bridle have evolved.

These modern horses tend to be warmbloods such as the German Hanoverian and Holstein, and the Dutch, Danish and Belgian warmbloods and of course last but not least the French horse that is today known as the French warmblood but originally included many thoroughbreds. Warmbloods are often warmed up using deeper outlines, or long and low stretch exercises (known in German as *losgelassenheit*). These methods differ from those of the classical methods and supple the muscles along the topline of the horse, flexing the muscles through the withers, neck and head to the mouth (Figure 5.1). The classical breeds naturally fit the classical outline. Their conformation, with the

Figure 5.1   This horse's energy is moving through the back and withers and he is swinging through the back and moving up to the bit.

head and neck up in front of the withers, has been developed through hundreds of years of breeding and positions you in such a way that you feel as if you are sitting in an armchair; it is so comfortable and easy to sit with the horse. Sport horses come with many advantages and a wide range of talents, but often need more suppling of the muscles around the shoulders to express such lightness and freedom. There are exceptions to every rule, but these differences explain the reasons for different forms of contact evolving.

Dressage opened up to more people after World War II when the Olympic Games welcomed women and non-army male riders, and a plethora of styles began to be seen at top-level riding throughout the world. New ideas were introduced from different schools of training such as the Hungarian, the

Prussian and the Scandinavian, all of which developed to suit the particular breeds/types of horses and the temperaments of the people riding them. Many of these different aspects of riding were blended to form the basis for modern dressage riding. For example, there was more emphasis on forming a bridge connecting the horse's hind legs, back and forehand into a type of bascule, like a jumping bascule, with the horse rounding his back up, the limbs carrying the weight better, energy moving through the withers and along the neck so that elevation can happen. Once this roundness is felt, the bascule is lifted up so that the horse moves upward and forward like the classical horse. This is seen in the competition warm-up arenas but the normal prescribed riding techniques being shown inside the competition arena have to follow the dressage rules. These rules often having been drawn up decades after successful riders of a specific era were using particular methods.

It is important to know both the classical and modern methods in order to ride dressage and for this reason I explain later in this chapter: 1) riding long and low exercises, 2) the half neck position, and 3) riding the horse in a deeper outline.

No horse should be stuck in a particular frame continually, it puts strain on his body, he should be ridden in different outlines during each training session so that the muscles are stretched and contracted, and that the horse develops the correct posture for dressage. This suppling resembles the training of any athlete, i.e. never adopting one posture continually but stretching, developing muscle and doing different exercises in order to achieve the ultimate aim of the sport in which they participate. Some horses are born with almost ideal conformation so that they appear to be on the bit even while munching hay. It is easier to train this sort of horse to accept contact, but every horse needs suppling for the ultimate outline to develop. If this is neglected, muscles will stiffen and resistances will appear; every horse must come to contact through correct riding, and the building up of a way of going that allows for correct contact to be established. It allows you to use discreet aids to streamline the power of the horse for the purposes you choose. The best advice is to stay flexible in your choice of methods. You are training an athlete, he is like a dancer or gymnast, he needs loosening, stretching, and toning, and contact gives you the means to achieve this. You must also understand the conformation of the horse. Use the classical way initially, but utilize the modern ways for short periods to help soften the horse if he does not respond well to it. The horse will tell you if he is happy, you will feel it in your hands, but if you have doubts, use different methods little and often. Never overdo anything, keep the horse soft and smooth, keep him moving, seeking the bit, and give him periods of rest on a long rein so that his muscles can recover.

The ultimate picture to focus on is the classical outline, which will put the horse in the ideal shape to move well. Horses do not eat the grass in the field in long and low positions – well, very rarely – and when they 'dance' at liberty they hold their heads and necks beautifully arched, freeing their limbs to float gracefully. The best way for the horse to move is as nature intended and so we should emulate nature to get the most from our dressage training. For example, horses free in fields never stick to the same outline for hours on end: they move and look around, eat grass, or snooze quietly, and so we should let horses move in different outlines during every schooling session so that their muscles do not become sore. Contact improves when the horse is allowed to stretch.

Contact acts as a barometer of a horse's training and each training stage brings new dimensions, new levels of lightness, new excitements, and new challenges. Facing these challenges builds trust between horse and rider. Contact contributes to trust in a unique way because there is an unseen, unknown quality to contact. It is not just the technique but the horse's willing-ness to work in self-carriage or submission. When the relationship between horse and rider has developed to this point, both partners will get the other out of trouble when mistakes are made, and to receive such loyalty from your horse is marvellous. Contact also has psychological and physical manifestations that go beyond the measurable. It is the harmony between horse and rider.

Some riders hold the reins so sweetly it resembles a brilliant musician playing a violin: such a gift cannot be taught, it is a talent given by God. Yet horses are ridden by masses of different people (different races, different body shapes and temperaments) and not just by a few with such natural ability. Techniques have developed to teach the rider what contact is, but many riders still find it hard to understand. This spurred me to ask questions about ways of teaching it. I want riders to know what it feels like to hold reins containing the energy of the horse, and more deep questions about this nudged me to ask even more questions. I fell back on the classical principles, but began to experiment. I began to investigate alternatives styles of contact, how to teach them, when to use them, and what types of horses they suited. The result was a conglomerate of experiences that I have outlined in this chapter. It is based on years of everyday teaching, applying the principles through practical application. Yet I returned to the classical method as it was the best way. I like the modern techniques, they have helped many horses and riders, but the classical way follows nature closely, every horse likes it, and that's good enough for me. This is not a judgemental statement, but one of personal observation and preference.

The Practice of Riding with Contact

I have divided the subject of contact into four steps, which I hope makes it easier for you. Each step has ideas, practical instruction, and observations. Perhaps you will read through each step quickly, referring to a section that is particularly applicable to you, and then read it again more thoroughly knowing improving means refining and applying the principles more deeply. Think about the effects of your riding, think about the reasons these effects are happening (cause and effect) check your position, study your horse's mouth and find bits he likes. You know he changes balance as he develops, and his needs also change. Think through riding situations and relate them to the hands and contact.

It is impossible to write about every riding or teaching situation, but I want you to be the best rider you can be. You will have to take the responsibility to think things through yourself (there is no escaping this reality no matter how many dressage lessons you have) and this principle applies to contact more than any other aspect of dressage. But I can help to improve your understanding; I want to get you riding better than you have ever ridden before and that is the purpose of writing this book. You may not train with the best trainers in the world, but concepts cannot be watered down and if you use your brain coupled with good practice it will be as if you have this facility. Ultimately, *you* are responsible. Ultimately, *you* are the one riding the horse. Ultimately, *you are on your own* when you enter the arena to compete. If you want to ride well you need to be brave. Remember, it takes not only ability and brawn but also brains to ride good dressage; use your brain and think through your riding sessions, especially with regard to contact. Have feeling hands that are joined to the horse.

Step One: Giving Your Horse a Mouth

Giving a horse a mouth means that the mouth is totally prepared for acceptance of the bit. It involves every part of his mouth, from fitting and selecting the bit, fitting the bridle, checking his teeth are in good condition and there are no sharp teeth, to preparing him to accept the weight of the rein in the rider's hands. Years ago it was a normal part of training horses when they were used for war, work, farming, sport, and as a means of transport. Indeed, for riders at the Spanish Riding School of Vienna it is, and always was, a priority. They spent many months studying details about tack and bits as apprentices and were required to pass tests with high percentage passes before they could continue into the second year of training. But today few people spend time giving their horses mouths.

It should be done in the early stages of training (and checked throughout the training) to ensure the horse comes to better contact. Such attention to detail makes the difference between quality and mediocre work but, because the horse's mouth is so sensitive, if we fail to get this part of the training right it can ruin every other aspect of the work.

SELECTING THE RIGHT BIT FOR YOUR HORSE

Check that your horse is wearing the right bit and that it fits well. You do not want him to worry about the bit, spit it out, or stick his tongue out of his mouth or over the bit. These reactions show his disgust and you want him to be happy.

Selecting the right bit for your horse is vital to ensure that he enjoys his bit as much as he would enjoy sucking a sweet. The bit is an instrument of training, not an instrument of torture. It makes no sense to use the bit as a punishment, horses enjoy being submissive, you should be friends, and they should enjoy the closeness between you that the bit brings.

To select the right bit study the horse's mouth. What size and shape is the tongue? How thick are his lips? What are the teeth like? Is there much room in his mouth to carry a bit? Make sure the bit fits exactly. If you do not know the correct size of bit required, try as many bits as you can until you find one that fits well; measuring the mouth piece of this bit between the bit rings will give you the size your horse needs. When you know these details, select a gentle dressage snaffle, e.g. a single-jointed German loose-ring snaffle, a lozenge bit, or a spatula bit like the French link snaffle; these are the bits used for dressage training. Bits permitted for dressage competition are kind bits and it is always advisable to go for the gentlest bit a horse will work well in because horses have mouths as sensitive as those of humans.

As well as the *correct fit*, you have to find a bit that a horse *likes*. Stay open-minded, select a couple of bits, make sure they fit the horse's mouth and then ride the horse in them to see how he reacts and how they feel. The horse will tell you if he is happy and comfortable, or unhappy and uncomfortable, with a particular bit.

Once I discover the bit a horse likes I stick to it, but if for any reason he stops accepting it, I change it for another. I might, for example, have to change from a lozenge bit to a single-jointed snaffle. Generally lozenge bits are excellent, most horses love them, the metal is rounded, the lozenge set at an angle that allows room for the tongue, and it gives precise feel on either side of the rein. They are designed to give a rider the facility to soften one rein so that action can be applied on one side of the bit without affecting the action on the other side, thus allowing precision communication with the mouth.

But some horses – those with thin tongues and small mouths – like a 'sloppy' bit and hate precision bits because there is limited room on either side of their tongues. In this case a horse would go better in a single-jointed snaffle. It is the classical dressage bit, and helps straightness as, if fitted well, it will sit centrally in the horse's mouth. Also the breeding of the modern sport horse has included Thoroughbred bloodlines and this has resulted in horses having smaller mouths, and for some reason these types prefer the lozenge bit. Whichever type of snaffle your horse likes, when the time comes for you to advance to the double bridle use the same style for the bradoon (the light jointed snaffle of the double bridle).

Most horses like to be ridden consistently in one bit, but there are those who like to change bits on a regular basis. For example, show jumpers and eventers might like to train in one bit and compete in another, and this applies to some dressage horses too. Some highly competitive-natured horses need a reminder to be obedient, that the rider is the boss. Bitting rules are not hard and fast, therefore, each horse must be treated as an individual.

Bitting the young horse

Horses never bitted before appreciate sweet treats such as treacle, honey, or molasses smothered over the bit to encourage them to take it. Strip the bridle down to the cheek pieces, the head piece and the bit and undo one cheek piece. Once you have gently manoeuvred the bit into the horse's mouth, quietly slide the head piece over the horse's head, and re-buckle the cheek piece to the bit ring. Too much strap work around his head might upset him initially. If he does get upset you can easily slip off the bridle, and try again once he settles. As soon as he is happy with the bit and bridle being put on and taken off, you can slip on the bridle without undoing the cheek pieces.

Next, stand beside him, give him a few treats and pet him, make much of him and tell him what a good boy he is, and then slip a headcollar over the bit and tie him up. Make sure he is tied to a piece of string attached to a tie ring so that if he gets frightened he can be untied quickly and he will not hurt himself. Stay beside him while he is tied up, until you can gradually lengthen the time he remains tied to the headcollar (but with a bit and bridle underneath), and never leave him unattended. I find that this training is a kind way of getting submission before you even start training. I was surprised to learn that just the training art of tying a horse up helped submission but then discovered that young stallions at the Portuguese School were left halter tied for periods of time, as were the young unbroken stallions of the Spanish School. It teaches good manners and encourages the first stages of obedience.

When I untie the horse I quietly slip off the headcollar and then I might feed a handful of mix in a bowl. This encourages the horse to open and close his mouth, and to chew the bit while eating. Gentle handling will also help a horse learn to accept and enjoy his bit, instead of being resistant to it and trying to spit it out, and it is part of the process of becoming obedient to the will of the rider.

Young horses also like basic snaffles like the straight bar made of nylon material, and they can be good to use for a short time while introducing the bit to the horse. However, they do not produce flexion in the same way as a jointed snaffle because there are not so many effects on the horse's mouth and they therefore have limited use for dressage. If you decide to use a key bit to start off a young horse use it for only a short time because horses get mouthy with this bit, the keys make them chew the bit too vigorously and they can develop a snaky tongue, sliding it back and forth.

Non-riders can be horrified when they consider the idea of placing bits in the mouths of horses but, as with so many things, it is not the bit that causes discomfort or damage but the hands manipulating the bit. And, it could be said that the bars of the horse's mouth have almost been designed to hold a bit. A bit correctly used by sensitive hands can influence the whole of a horse's body, from the hindquarters to the poll, to produce a stunning and beautiful picture of lightness, beauty and harmony. Study the propensity for the forces of the horse's energy, his muscle structure, his sensitivity and strength, to be controlled through the bit – it is phenomenal.

BASIC WORK IN-HAND

In-hand work is a wonderful way to get to know your horse. Both young and experienced horses benefit and it is simple for the handler to do. You feel close to the horse, you can see his mouth and observe reactions and, in turn, the horse senses your closeness and feels your concern for his welfare. He knows you respect him and his confidence grows.

In-hand work gives the impression that not much is happening but, in fact, there is a lot going on. If you have never done this work before I strongly recommend that you have a go, and I am sure both you and your horse will enjoy it. It is good for a young horse because it teaches him the rein weight aids and the feel of the bit in his mouth, and it is good for freshening up the mouths of experienced horses, especially if they are resistant or hard mouthed. If you

Figure 5.2   The first stages of work in-hand.

have done all your training correctly but the horse should really accept the bridle better, simple flexions in-hand will help.

Basic work in-hand can be performed with young horses or novices to help them understand and be happy with the bit. This aspect might have been missed from their previous training. Start by buckling the reins onto the snaffle and take the reins over the horse's head, holding them in one hand close to the horse's chin; the chin is sensitive to touch and so lightly touching the chin with the knuckles of your hand nearest the horse will be effective in asking the horse to move forward into walk (Figure 5.2). Do this with a forward action, a gentle nudge. Walk alongside him and remember that the horse moves more quickly and covers more ground than you and so you will need to stride out.

To encourage forwardness you may need to stand near the horse's head to start him off, but you will find you will be able to step backwards until you are level with his withers once he is walking forwards. You can use the voice to encourage him as well and, if necessary, give him a gentle tap on the shoulder, either with the hand or with a short stick if he is happy with the stick, at the same time as you press your knuckles into his chin. (Figure 5.3)

When you ask him to halt, give feather-light squeezes (snowflake soft) on both reins, most horses will not need more than this pressure and, if they do, maintain it only for an instant and then revert to the gentle squeezes. If the horse is not getting the message, or is a little strong, place yourself close in to his shoulder and lean your weight into it, you will find he will understand. This is also the best position to be in if a horse misbehaves (Figure 5.4). When teaching the halt in-hand, you can also say 'whoa' – I say this as 'wha-hooo,' and horses

Figure 5.3 Use your hand or a short stick to give the forward aid on the horse's shoulder. After the horse responds to this forward aid, you can progress to using a short stick where your leg would be positioned whilst still working him in-hand, which familiarizes the horse with the leg aids before he is backed.

seem to like this and know to stop – but you will find it soon becomes unnecessary to speak because as you are close to the horse, he will follow your body language, and you will move as one.

Start in walk and halt and progress to walk/trot transitions when you both feel happy and confident. Put the reins back over his head, and move your working position from standing next to the horse's head to near the withers.

Figure 5.4 Always put safety first; be aware of your body positioning so that you do not get knocked by the horse's front legs. Here the handler is placing her body into the side of the horse as the filly gets playful.

Some horses may like you to be flexible and move your position from his head to the girth area in order to understand what you want. Cater to a horse's needs and his confidence will grow. Know that he is happy to walk off with the lightest tap on the shoulder and stop with the lightest flutter on the reins. This is enough for him at the initial stage. Once he understands I progress to putting the reins over his head and, even though I am working on the ground, using them as if I am riding. I position the outside rein over the withers and down his side by the girth until it is level with the bit on the side of the horse from which I am working. I keep the inside rein loose and in the hand furthest away from the horse. Again, remain flexible. For example, with some youngsters I have held both reins up by the withers, and with others I have held the outside rein as a steady contact and the inside one with lighter contact. Whichever way I hold the reins, my aim is to introduce the horse to the outside rein, to a contact rein, to a long rein, and a loose rein. This is the purpose of this initial in-hand work.

This work is simple to do even for a beginner, and if you have not done this work before don't worry, the horse will soon understand what you want. As soon as a horse is happy with this work in walk, the energetic trainer can do it in trot. Make sure you are wearing comfortable shoes that cover your feet well for safety's sake, or boots that are comfortable to run in. The same rules for the work in walk apply but be aware that running with a horse in trot in an arena surface that drags on your feet will require a high level of fitness.

Work in-hand is such a joy. It has a unique quality that is beyond explanation, the effects are minute yet spectacular, and it sums up that dressage adage: less means more.

I have always taught a young horse to go forward and halt in-hand in order to bring him to submission before I back him and start his ridden schooling.

FLEXIONS IN-HAND

This work can be done in a snaffle, or a double bridle, and is best done when the horse is progressing to Elementary standard. I prefer to do most flexions in halt and for only about five minutes at a time during a short training period over a few weeks, and I would only refer back to this work for a specific purpose such as a horse stiffening against the hand, particularly if he has a history of overcoming this fault only through flexion work. This applies to a horse who is well trained in the basics in every way but his self-carriage and acceptance of the bit could be better. It is a *very small* part of the training, and yet it can be extra-ordinarily beneficial.

Stand in front, or on the nearside of your horse, hold the reins as you would when riding and feel the horse's reaction to the bit/s through your hands. If you are using a double bridle, feel his reaction to both the bradoon and the curb. If he is stronger on one side than the other, you can soften on the harder side whilst keeping hold of the lighter side in a steady contact. As you are so close to the horse, you can feel, and see, his reactions. As soon as he is happy with you 'feeling' his mouth you can position his head through the poll to one side, return to the original position, feel again the horse's mouth in your hands, and then position to the other side. The positioning increments can be as small as ¼–½ in (approx. ½ cm) or as wide as 6 in–1 ft (15–30 cm), but the smaller the better.

You can also give your horse treats to reward him while you are doing this work, but do not over-treat him or he will start rummaging in your pockets and stop concentrating on the work in-hand. But do give him plenty of pats and tell him what a good boy he is. I find horses seem to really enjoy work in-hand and it encourages a horse to love the bit.

Step Two: Practical Ways to Achieve Contact

The classical ways to bring your horse up to the contact are by the preparatory work of lungeing with correctly fitted side reins, work in-hand, and riding with equal contact on both reins with a rein that is held in the hand with an elastic feel and the open and indirect rein. Other techniques evolve from these basics such as the unilateral half-halt, inside leg to outside rein, and the half-halts on the inside rein to soften, and on the outside rein to control the speed. All these methods will be discussed.

STRAIGHT IN FRONT OF THE WITHERS
When a horse is ridden straight, this straightness comes through the body, the withers and neck to the head and, until suppleness through inside bend is

established, we keep the shoulders, head and neck straight in front of the withers. This is logical, it is like riding a bicycle, to go in a straight line we keep the handle bars square in front, otherwise the bike wiggles all over the place. The same thing happens to the horse if we ride with too much inside bend, we lose the straightness through the head and neck, and through the quarters swinging away from the direction of the movement. The horse has no collarbone, the backbone is attached to the front of the horse by a cradle of muscles that have to be stabilized to create a secure base to work from, so that inside bend can be achieved in future training. Without this stability the horse will bend and contort himself against the rider's will, bending too much to evade correction, or stiffening, or curling away from the contact.

The horse is first taught to accept contact on both reins with the head and neck straight in front of the withers, and this gives the stable base. All schools emphasize this stability. Bend through the body is taught gradually in a way that the horse can assimilate through his body; he accepts the control of contact by seeking the bit through the activity from the hindquarters driving him forward to the bit.

How to achieve equal contact on both reins

The straightness of equal contact starts simply by riding the horse with his head and neck straight in front of his withers, i.e. when the line of the crest runs straight from his withers to the centre of the space between his ears. Look down at his shoulders, if you can see one eye but not the other, or his ears are tipped (one lower than the other) or you feel he is 'wiggling' in front of the withers so that it feels like you are riding a bicycle without handlebars, or he clamps his inside jaw tight against softening actions of the hand aids, then it is likely that there is too much inside bend and not enough acceptance of the outside contact. Correct it by softening on the outside rein gently and straightening the head before the body. Then check that you are sitting square to axis and that your legs are hanging down underneath your hips, because if one leg is behind the girth and the other is forward you will push the quarters away, and lose the horse through the withers. Also, if both legs are too far behind the girth you will limit your control of the front end, and have no sensitivity for slight inside bend through corners. Sitting square to axis in the correct classical position will avoid such errors (see Chapter 2).

Your shoulders and hips must be level and you must look in the direction in which the horse is moving; imagine a string coming out of your tummy button, if it runs in a straight line along the line of the horse's neck to his poll you know you are sitting correctly. Make sure the weight of the reins in your hands is the same (except for a young horse that needs correction), that your shoulders and elbows are positioned to ensure the reins are held in the same way, and that there is no blocking through one elbow or shoulder caused by locking an elbow or stiffening a shoulder, because it can affect the equality of the contact on both reins. Keep your elbows soft so that you can feel the contact through the wrist, hand, and fingers. If you can achieve all this you will be looking good!

Don't be too tough on yourself if you are a little crooked in your body, causing crookedness in the horse, because nobody is totally symmetrical, we are not statues but flesh and blood. But do be aware of your errors, correct them, check that the feels your are receiving from the horse are the same as those you receive when he is going well, and check that the horse's shoulders are in front of the withers. It is also important to ride on straight lines frequently; do not ride endless circles, but ride circles to straight lines. Practise figure riding and make sure you use the whole arena. Remember that although we do straighten a horse with lateral work, inside leg to outside rein and other dressage techniques, the reality is we ride our horse straight, and our aim is to ride the horse straight with equal contact on both reins.

THE OPEN AND INDIRECT REIN

These reins boost straightness, but should be used with discretion. For example, introduce them to the young horse by changes of rein along the diagonal, and later by turns down the centre line. *Always* make changes of direction by positioning your shoulders and hips along the new directional line. This change of direction should be a flowing movement, and can be precipitated by placing more weight on the inside stirrup bringing the inside leg *slightly* forwards. A young horse's typical response might be to veer off, pulling to the outside, the movement escaping through the outside shoulder, and such a horse may need a little help to negotiate the turn. Keep the weight on the inside stirrup as explained, but with a relaxed soft inside leg, and apply the outside leg behind the girth to bring him up through the outside shoulder so that he is not falling on the forehand.

When executing these turns, the inside rein is the open rein and is used together with the outside rein, which is the indirect rein. *Always* open the inside rein for the young horse by moving the inside hand to the side but making sure it opens like an opening door and does not pull backward. The indirect rein and the knuckles of your outside hand snuggle against the outside of the horse's withers. The opening of the inside rein can vary from an exaggerated opening for a young horse to a discreet 'turning of the key', i.e. a turning of the wrist to bring the thumb towards the inside of the withers thus turning the rein very subtly outwards. However, for most horses it is easier to perform this opening with the hand held with the thumb on top so that you maintain the straight line to a soft elbow, and you keep the open rein to just ¼–½ in (approx. 1 cm).

When the outside rein lies snugly against the outside of the withers it acts as an indirect rein to keep the shoulder over to the opposite side. If it is held slightly away from the withers it helps stop the horse bending too much to the inside, or tipping his head to the inside.

My advice is to feel the flow, feel the turns, feel the changes of direction, and ride them in a simple way following the principle of *always sitting square to axis, never pulling on the inside rein, putting the weight onto the stirrup on the side of the turn you are making, and looking in the direction of that turn.* This is the simplest and best way to ride.

LATERAL AND VERTICAL FLEXION

This is the positioning through the poll: vertical flexion is when the horse brings his nose down from the poll, and lateral flexion is when he positions his head sideways to the left or right. 'Flexion' is the classical term used to cover both vertical and lateral bend through the poll, combined with the acceptance of the bit, and also covers self-carriage relating to the head carriage of the horse. However, today's riders tend to use the word 'bend' more than 'flexion' but I mention it in this chapter so that you have an understanding of the differences. In other parts of the book I refer to both bend and flexion as 'bend' unless it would be confusing.

Lateral bend is normally slight, i.e. ½–1 or 2 in (1–5 cm), *very slight*, and this bend is supported by the leg on the same side as the bend being placed softly on the girth, or 1–2 in (2–5 cm) in front of the girth. This soft and relaxed support by the inside leg on the girth asks for bend (normally inside bend), and the positioning of the leg slightly forward of the girth (level with the first rib) asks for bend through the body.

Lateral and vertical bend are both related to contact. Vertical bend can be used separately (as explained in the section about keeping the head and neck straight in front of the withers on pages 169–170). With vertical flexion the horse flexes so that his nose is the lowest point and his poll is the highest point. It is often combined with lateral flexion for bending exercises, softening through the poll, or for inside bend. Poor vertical flexion will be improved by lateral flexion exercises.

You will find that the process of riding the exercises for bend is easy and will automatically lead to flexion.

Flexion exercises

1. Begin with the basics as explained in the previous pages, i.e. encourage the horse to like the contact, teach him to understand stepping forward into the hand aids, the turn-of-direction hand through the open and indirect rein, the stop hand through work in-hand, and give and takes on the outside rein to regulate speed.
2. Introduce inside-leg-to-outside-rein-exercises through turns and on circles, as explained in Chapter 4.
3. Soften the inside rein keeping a steady contact on the outside rein. Think of the outside rein as though it is electricity: when you walk into a room and flick the switch, the electricity flows through the wires to turn the light bulb on, and this is the connection you want through the outside rein; the bulb's wattage dictates the intensity of the light that comes through, and each horse will have a different intensity of feel in the outside rein. The

outside rein contact is kept steady and still unless there are specific reasons to do otherwise: for example, to position to the outside, or to soften it to ask for a half-halt to communicate to the horse to soften on that side of the bit or to prepare for a transition.

4. Ride a corner by approaching it with slight outside bend, straightening the horse before you reach it, taking inside bend through the corner, then support the inside flexion with a soft inside leg positioned slightly forward of the girth in order to ask for bend through the horse's first rib, and straightening the horse again when you are travelling along a straight line either to the next corner or the long side of the arena.

5. Flexions can be done in halt in a similar way to flexions in-hand, except they are more exaggerated. They help soften a stiff poll. This exercise focuses on acceptance of the bit on both sides of the mouth. Come to a halt and sit quietly and then very gently position the horse to one side. If positioning to the right, soften through the left elbow to allow for the extra bend to the right and follow it through with the right hand positioning the horse's head more to the right. These flexions can be as little as 1–3 in (2.5–7.5 cm) or as much as 1 ft–1 ft 6 in (30–45 cm) approximately. The feeling is soft and gentle. Photo 5.5 illustrates this flexion well. Do not overdo this exercise, no more than half a minute on each side, bringing the horse's head back to the central straight line before flexing to the other side.

6. Ride exercises like the V-shaped pattern by riding from one quarter marker to X and then to the next quarter marker, showing change of bend through X.

7. Ride loops showing change of bend to practise lateral flexions. Use circles to practise softening on the inside rein to a steady outside rein to encourage a softer inside contact, and a jaw yielding more to the inside will give better vertical flexion. If you ride deep (see pages 180–182) do not worry if it is very deep if, when you put your legs on, the horse comes up through the shoulder and poll, and is still in front of the leg and not behind the movement.

8. Ride changes of lateral flexions interspersed with the placing of the head and neck straight in front of the withers. Ride the flexions and the straightening for at least a few strides, or much longer, but resist swinging the

horse's head from side to side. This will result in him getting dizzy, and it does not put him on the rein but takes him off it.

THE UNILATERAL HALF-HALT

The unilateral half-halt is used to straighten the horse to accept the bit on both sides. It is the next step from riding the horse straight in front of the withers and the classical way of teaching inside leg to outside rein, although it is more specific.

Halt your horse, take up both reins and feel which rein the horse accepts more, i.e. the rein that he takes more contact on (it might feel stiff and resistant, or just have a nice elastic feel in the hand). It will feel heavier than the rein on his hollow side. Until a horse is straightened he is slightly banana shaped, i.e. he has a natural tendency to bend to one side and resists bending to the other side. But this is the aim of straightening: to supple both sides, straightening out this banana shape

Figure 5.5 Bending through the poll to the inside at halt.

and encouraging the horse to accept the contact equally on both sides through the body and not just a positioning of the head and neck straight in front of the withers (although this would have started the straightening process).

Let us assume your horse is stiff to the right and hollow to the left, he will have an inclination to overbend to the left and to resist bend to the right, he will be heavier on the right rein, and try to escape from the contact on the left rein by allowing the movement to escape through the shoulders and neck.

Take up both reins, gently position the neck as straight as nature allows, keeping both reins at an equal distance from the neck, and give and take on the stiff right rein only. This giving and taking may only need to be light or, for a resistant horse, it may need to be a little stronger for a few gives and takes. You have to make him understand that he has to stop hanging onto the right side of the bit. Ideally, apply this give and take by squeezing with the fingers as if you were squeezing out a sponge and then releasing the squeeze, or the squeeze can be as light as a feather flutter if your horse is light on the reins, but if a more definite feel is needed, and often this applies to inexperienced horses, open the angle of your elbow and move your hand towards the horse's mouth by at least 1–6 in (2.5–15 cm) as you release the squeeze, and then return the elbow to its original position as you squeeze.

The horse will soon start to lighten, to soften his feel on the right side of the bit. You may feel him chew his bit and soften his poll, and he will slightly lower his poll vertically. This means he has yielded to your requests on the right side of his jaw and you will find he comes into better contact on the left side. When you feel more contact on the left side, maintain the contact and keep the rein still; do not fiddle with it, do nothing. The horse might take a stronger hold on the right side again and if he does you will have to repeat the exercise.

Do this exercise in halt initially to give the horse time to understand what is being asked of him. It is usual for horses to respond positively after a few efforts, and then you are ready to do the unilateral half-halts on the circle on the left rein because the horse is stiffer on the right side. You can incorporate inside leg to outside rein on the circle and a softening on the rein to soften the horse's acceptance of the bit, and this gives the horse a good quality base from which he is encouraged to do well. He will feel pleased with himself and this encourages him to submit to our will without really realizing it. It is much better that he gives his will freely thinking that it was his idea in the first place. This is a subtle way of teaching a horse to accept the will of the rider willingly and without resistance or because he feels he has no option, i.e. submission, and we should never forget that teaching the horse to accept the bit is teaching submission. Next, change the rein to circle on the right rein. You may need to hold the left rein slightly away from the neck as an open rein, and be discreet with the inside rein half-halts so that you do not lose the horse's straightness by the movement being lost through the outside shoulder. The aim is to get a more genuinely elastic feel on both reins so that it is more equal; this will be achieved by degrees through the horse's willingness to soften to the half-halts, which are through the hand only unless the energy needs refreshing, in which case apply the leg aids to ask the horse to step forwards more to the bit. But if the energy is flowing through well and you are sitting square to axis there is no need to create more energy than is needed, because you will not be able to contain it in the hand. You can ensure you are streamlining the energy by riding transitions.

Once the horse understands that the softening on the stiff rein means yielding on that side of the jaw, and accepting the contact on the hollow side better, you can begin to bring in unilateral half-halts while riding on straight lines going large. Now the exercise begins to bear real fruit. Initially, it is best to keep this softening work to the stiff side only, no matter if on the right or left rein, even when asking for a slowing-of-speed half-halt that would normally be restricted to the outside rein. Check that the horse understands your instructions clearly. Horses do normally pick up these communications quickly because they are more intelligent than many would give them credit for.

As a result of these unilateral half-halts, the horse immediately comes into better vertical flexion, but the longer-term benefit is that he will be able to hold his frame in better vertical flexion over longer periods of time. You will feel him becoming steady and quiet on the bit and the feel will be equal on both reins, and then one day you will realize that the horse has swapped his stiff and hollow sides, that is instead of moving bilaterally he will stiffen on the side that was originally his hollow side, and hollow on the side that was his stiff side. Is he doing that naughty schoolboy act again? Not really, it is a normal physiological reaction to the straightening exercises. Give him a pat and laugh it off; you will soon have true acceptance of the bit on both sides of the horse's mouth. This is a sign that the horse is progressing and you can be pleased with yourself and your horse. (Figures 5.6a and b)

Figures 5.6a and b   a) I am holding my hands wide apart and bending the mare to the inside to loosen her; she is blocking the bend through the ribcage to the inside. b) The mare is now up through the poll with the head and neck in a classical position.

MODERN METHODS OF ACHIEVING CONTACT

Some of the modern methods are used purely for short bursts of time within a training session (e.g. the long and low exercises, and the half-neck position).

Long and low

'Long and low' is the well-known German method of loosening the horse. In German it is called *losgelassenheit*, and is also known as warming up. The following is how Ferdi Eilberg describes long and low.

'How you ride *losgelassenheit* depends on the horse's personality and his standard of training. For example, with young horses as much as 90 per cent of a training session can be devoted to this phase. A supple and calm horse would start in walk on a long rein, usually for five to ten minutes, before being trotted around the arena perhaps in turns and circles. The canter is normally included, but for a hot horse it is better not to insist that he stays in walk when he wants to get on with things and go forwards. Go off in working trot and let the horse use some of his excess energy, and then when he needs a breather he will be happy to relax and walk on a long rein. With a trained horse *losgelassenheit* normally takes 25–40 per cent of the training session ... Most horses begin with walk on a long rein for about ten minutes ... During *losgelassenheit* I ask the horse to stretch his head and neck down so that the muscles along his top line become loosened and suppled. To ask for this stretching the horse is ridden with an extra bit of "roundness" onto the bridle and then the rider lets the reins slip through the fingers and as this happens the horse will want to stretch down.' (*Pathfinder Dressage*, Penny Hillsdon: 'The German Way', p.77 – J.A. Allen, 2000).

Long and low is used to supple the horse in preparation for serious work, it should not be used continuously or it will tend to put the horse on the forehand, go against his natural way of moving and may disconnect him in front of the withers giving you the feeling that there is no control of the front of the horse. Having his head hovering just above the arena surface for hours at a time is neither good for a horse's breathing nor for his overall balance. This method should come with a safety warning to riders not familiar with its dangers that it should never be done for too long periods.

The best gait in which to practise long and low is the working trot. Use it for a short time integrating it into other exercises such as free walk on a long rein, canter to trot transitions, and blend in long and low trot exercising. Because this is a continental method, these riders are very familiar with it but, perhaps because of a lack of understanding or communication, other nations use this loosening method too much during training, and thereby undo the benefits. Introduce it into active work, and combine it with the proper contact work.

Long and low suits many horses, but not the horse who is not built well up in front of the withers, i.e. if he tends to be on his forehand. To judge this for yourself, look at your horse on flat, level ground and observe him standing with his weight distributed over all four feet. How does the point of his croup relate to the top of his shoulder? Are they level or is the shoulder lower? If it is lower, I would avoid long and low exercising since, as stated, this work does put the horse on the forehand more. For this type of horse use the classical walk on a long rein, and up and forward contact riding. If your horse is built with his forehand in proportion to the hindquarters, carries himself well up in front of the saddle when moving, and has the type of conformation referred to as 'up in front of the wither', then you can safely use long and low under the conditions explained above.

The half-neck position

The half-neck position is a modern way of taking long and low, combining it with a deeper head and neck position, and using it as a warming up exercise, but without the dangers of putting the horse on the forehand to such a marked degree. Ask the horse for a rounder outline and to bring his head and neck down a little deeper, but no deeper than the bottom of his chest. The half-neck position lies between the deep and long-and-low positions.

Modern competitive riders favour this half-neck position; it seems to suit most types of horses and is closer to a horse's natural head and neck carriage. A horse can be asked to bring his head and neck up higher to a deep position, and then up again to the classical contact position. This relies on a rider's ability to differentiate between the feels of the different head and neck positions, on good riding and the correct use of the rider's legs and hands to ride the horse up to the contact. It teaches the horse to be up in front of the bridle with the energy coming from the hindquarters, through the back, to the hand. It establishes softness through the back and teaches the horse to respond to the leg, seat and hand aids. It has many advantages but, again, for safety's sake it should only be used for short periods. It is better to go slowly and to teach the horse correctly so that he develops as an athlete, in balance and in harmony with the rider.

Riding deep

Riding deep lies between the correct contact position and the half-neck position. It helps horses that stiffen the muscles through the shoulder and block over the withers; it lifts the muscles up thus enhancing the rounding of the topline. It especially suits horses that perhaps are a little too much up in front of the withers or those that resist coming softly onto the contact in the classical way. In these circumstances it can be beneficial in getting the horse to come onto the bit more softly but you need to ensure that the horse works off the leg aids well and does not move with his nose stuck down, refusing to lift his head and neck when you put the leg and seat on to ask for a higher head carriage. If a horse moves in true deepness, he *will* respond to the leg.

I would advise alternating riding deep with the correct classical outline; it works well when combined with different outlines. For example, start walk on a long rein, ride forward into the half-neck position, ride the horse deeper for a short period, and then ride him up to the contact. If on a particular occasion you find that your horse is resistant, you can always use this deep position for longer periods, but I would advise you to give the horse breathing spaces on a long rein.

The advantage of riding deep is that you can do all the movement exercises and all general riding as if riding on a contact rein, and it keeps the horse on the aids and soft on the rein. However you cannot do all these different exercises when riding long and low, or with the half-neck position. So if you have a spooky horse, or a horse resistant to the contact (either because of his conformation, or because he is nervous) riding deep is a good option. You can then alternate riding deep with a slightly higher head and neck position, using the leg aids to ask for a lift of 2–4 or 5 in (5–10 or 12.5 cm) depending on the needs of the horse and it should bring the same softness, and acceptance of the bridle continues through. If it does not, revert to riding deep, and then start alternating it with other head and neck positions again. In fact, riding deep follows on from the classical idea that if the horse holds back energy, or tightens on the rein, you ride 1–2 in (2.5–5 cm) deeper (with the poll lower), refresh the gait and then ride the horse up and forward again. Riding deep is a more pronounced form of this classical riding concept. It is beneficial providing it is not taken to the extreme.

There is an escalation of this type of contact riding throughout Europe, and it does seem to work well for the warmbloods (particularly if they are hot), who are built with the withers set well up in front of the body, and for riders proficient in this technique.

Generally, riding deep is combined with using draw reins, which seems to be a modern trend that many competition riders are following and it cannot be denied that some results are good. I do not favour using the draw reins as a continual form of achieving contact because it goes against classical principles of training, and against nature, but I do use them for specific reasons at specific times. Riding deep should be done sympathetically without artificial aids but by the correct use of the hand, and this works well.

Some riders worry their horse is moving too deep thinking it puts the horse behind the bit, but this is not true. Providing the horse is genuinely in front of the leg, and rises up to the correct classical contact when the seat and leg are applied then it is correct. It is better to be deep in this correct way than too high and above the contact, and if a horse stiffens for whatever reason it is better to soften him to a deep outline where he will feel happy, otherwise he will get stiffer: his head will go up, he will become spooky, his back muscles will stiffen and drop down instead of rounding up under the weight of the rider, and it will be impossible for the horse to engage his hind legs actively underneath him. He will struggle with balance and forwardness, the steering will go wonky, the poll will tighten and, worse still, he could become disobedient. The next time you worry about your horse being over-bent worry instead about him being above the contact. The amount of time any horse can be precisely on the contact is not long, especially horses not up to Advanced standard. This explains why self-carriage should be taught early on. It refreshes contact and gives the horse freedom to express his gaits as nature intended.

CONTACT REIN, LONG REIN, LOOSE REIN

When training a horse to work on the contact you aim towards the first classical principle of the horse accepting the rein in three outlines in the working gaits.

1. The horse moving in walk, trot, and canter on a contact rein.
2. The horse moving in walk, trot, and canter on a long rein.
3. The horse moving in walk, trot, and canter on a loose rein.

Remember, a long rein is not a loose rein. Check your understanding of these definitions.

There is definite contact with a contact rein but *the amount of weight required on the rein can vary* with each horse from just a little more than the basic weight of the reins themselves to a stretched elastic feel. If the horse is not truly up to the contact the energy cannot power through as effectively as it might, rather like a boat with sails not trimmed to harness the wind and propel it forwards. Similarly, a rider harnesses the natural energy created in the hind legs through the contact. This explains why it is so important to know the difference between the different feels on the rein given by contact, long and loose reins. Only then can the horse be corrected if he backs off the bridle or drops the rein, in other words he is not working through to the rein enough. These two photos illustrate this point (Figures 5.7a and b).

A long rein is a rein with a little contact and a loose rein is a rein that hangs loose, normally to the buckle of the reins. Many riders like to start with contact and long reins first, and progress to loose-rein work once obedience is bedded in; this all adds up to horse and rider having greater confidence in each other.

If you have a spooky horse and are riding on a long rein do not worry that you have no control, because you can always reel him in and gather up the reins quickly. Do not be hesitant about riding on a long rein, you already give the horse rest periods of walk on a loose rein, just introduce trot on a long rein first, and then canter when you feel confident. I am always amazed that when all else fails simple work on a long rein will rectify bit resistances, inducing even the most reluctant horse to yield and come on the bit. If you give a horse freedom, he will respect you for trusting him and horses need respect as much as humans.

Figures 5.7a and b   a) This horse is dropping the rein and not working through her back correctly, and so energy is not streamlining through to the bit. b) The horse is now rounding through her back better in a good trot tempo but she could still be working to the rein better, although the picture is pleasing, and there could be more energy.

DOS AND DON'TS FOR CONTACT WORK

If a horse stiffens against your leg by stiffening the centre of his body, or wriggles away from it through the shoulder, bring your inside leg a little forward of the girth by 1–3 in (2.5–5 cm), and bend him to the inside a little more. If he is unstable in front of the withers, bend him a little to the outside with your outside leg becoming the inside leg and apply it a little further forward than the 3 in (5 cm). Establish a softer acceptance of the outside rein, then position him centrally through the poll with equal rein pressure, and then re-establish the true inside bend again, placing your inside leg forward by 1–3 in (2.5–5 cm) again to ask for inside bend, and bend him through the poll slightly (¼–½ in [approx. 1 cm] is often enough). He should now become more relaxed with your leg aids.

It is also important to remember that we humans are usually too busy with our hands and have a tendency to fiddle, which can also contribute to crookedness. Be sure of what you are doing with your hands and why; use them for a specific purpose, and then keep them still again.

Horses can use their hollow and stiff sides to exacerbate this crookedness in order to resist you; be aware of this and, if it happens, correct quietly but firmly and with a positive attitude.

Horses can be like naughty little schoolboys who love to stick their tongue out at authority and once you begin to progress with their training they seem to go through a tricky-teenager period when they will find any way they can to get away from knuckling down to the work at hand, and avoiding the contact is one of these evasions. You suss one evasion, and they come up with another, but if you are quick to react, and quick to correct quietly and firmly, you will find they stop resisting (Figures 5.8a and b). If you find it difficult to assess feels and situations quickly – and this is often the case until you are experienced – you will still know when things are going wrong and so ride on a long rein, think it through, try a different exercise, and return to the one that was causing problems. If you are still not able to identify the problem, think about it at home, think about your weight distribution and the exercise itself, e.g. is it too difficult, or did you ride it incorrectly, and I am sure you will be able to figure out the answer (Figures 5.9a and b). In fact, errors fall into stereotypical categories, and once you have an idea of what they all are, and you understand the character of your own horse, you will begin to develop the ability to think through your feels.

Figures 5.8a and b   a) This mare sometimes gets stubborn and resists and here she is above the bit. To resolve this she is halted, the contact is held lightly but steadily and the rider waits until she submits to the feel of the weight of the rein. This seems to work for some horses especially those who are established in their work and understand contact but who perhaps try it on. It gives the rider a simple and effective way of overcoming resistance. b) Here we see the same mare who has submitted to the contact through this simple exercise.

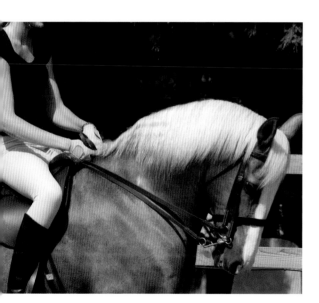

Figures 5.9a and b   a) Here the little palomino mare is evading by coming behind the vertical and b) she has capitulated and come onto the vertical.

Note that this rider uses a shorter stirrup than the dressage rider and we considered this way of riding suited horse and rider best; Annie shows this horse successfully and the wide big-moving mare fits a showing saddle better than a dressage one.

Draw reins and gadgets

As stated earlier, many people believe in the use of draw reins and gadgets to establish contact and there is no doubt that when handled correctly this equipment can assist this training. The problems arise, however, when they are used in a forceful and overbearing way and are used continuously to over-bend a horse into unnatural shapes for the sake of absolute control. Today people expect animals to be treated with compassion and choose to speak out against the misuse of gadgets. If these views are made known they will filter down from the highest to the lowest levels of training, to grass roots level. The best way to care for the horse is to follow the correct training methods, to say no to forceful trainers, to say no to forceful methods, and to express disgust when we see horses being cruelly ridden in any situation. Old-fashioned continental riders had a saying, 'The draw rein is like razors in the hands of a monkey.' It is a sobering thought, and one that makes a rider think about the importance of following correct methods of riding.

Step Three: Encouraging Lightness and Submission

There is an extraordinary X factor to contact that results in lightness and harmony between horse and rider that goes beyond explanation. Some horses have a natural ability to come light in the hand, others take longer and require patience from the trainer, but all are capable of good acceptance of contact. Some horses like coming on the bit more than others and have the character for submission, although they may lack the competitive X factor, and we cannot judge the horse who is more difficult to train to submission by the length of time it takes to teach him.

Working together is the true mark of submission, since it requires two to tango, you need to work in a partnership with the horse, respect him, like him and want the best for him, and these attitudes will overcome even the most reluctant horse. But it is more than just a simple partnership. A rider also needs humility to understand the nuances of submission. It takes wisdom and compassion to train a horse, it is more than cause and effect, more than submission/dominance; it is unity of purpose between horse and rider, and this unity can never exist unless it is accompanied by love.

The horse is so generous he can teach humans generosity but the rider has the brains and guides the horse to a higher level of thinking. We should never look down on his intelligence but seek ways to nudge him towards his own form of thinking within his dressage training, for example when teaching the walk-to-canter exercise. Do not dictate to the horse but ride him in a way that prompts the right reaction, that of him seeking to please you with the correct result. This mutual respect for each other's strengths, and understanding of each other's weaknesses, is best reflected in contact, because it leads to self-carriage and submission, and marks dressage as an extraordinary form of expression between man and beast.

All the different outlines offer options to enhance a horse's throughness to the bit, his natural energy flows freely forward to give you a natural force you can harness, an energy field going forward within the horse's frame. This force is like the wind that fills the sails of a sailing boat; the natural force of the wind propels the boat forwards, it is not driven by man-made energy from a man-made machine. The boat does not create the wind, nature creates the wind, and the sailor steers the boat into the wind, and trims his sails to make the most of this natural force to move the boat forwards. The same is true of the horse, we do not create the energy, the horse has natural energy, but we trim the horse with our leg and hand aids to make the most of that energy, and contact comes into play in this process. No amount of cajoling, prodding, or pushing can create energy from the horse, God have him natural energy, and our task is to streamline it.

The bit helps contain energy along with the seat, the horse loves to express his energy joyfully in dance, and you direct this joyfulness through training. First he is taught to move freely carrying the weight of a rider, and then the expression of his energy is fine-tuned by letting some out, by containing some, and by altering the outline of the horse to accommodate his natural way of going in the gaits and the different tempos. Contact is the key to these forces, which is why it is so important to study contact in depth, and to develop feel, good hands, and a good seat – all affect our connection with the horse. Contact connects the horse's hindquarters to our hands; this connection gives submission, direction, lightness and harmony to condition the horse for self-carriage (Figure 5.10).

Figure 5.10   Giving the inside rein to connect to the outside contact and encourage straightness, lightness and conditioning for self-carriage.

CONDITIONING THE HORSE FOR SELF-CARRIAGE

Developing self-carriage can start shortly after the horse has been backed, but normally begins at the Preliminary stage. Once the horse is happy to accept contact, be generous and give the rein towards his mouth a few inches; this refreshing can happen often or infrequently, depending on the character of the horse. If he is bullish – and competitive-spirited horses often are – teach obedience to the contact before overdoing self-carriage exercises but if he is easy-going, giving with the rein to encourage self-carriage can occur frequently. Self-carriage is expressed in Novice-level competition when the rider is asked to push the reins down the horse's neck while in canter. The horse should remain in the same outline, demonstrating self-

Figure 5.11 Giving and retaking the reins in working canter. The horse should stay in the same rhythm, balance and outline.

carriage and that he is not resting on the rein (Figure 5.11).

Horses have a tendency to use your hands as props, if you are not careful this can disintegrate into the horse going on the forehand and becoming insensitive to the hand. Self-carriage overcomes all these dangers.

First, condition the horse to self-carriage by giving the inside rein towards his mouth, this can be done to a *marked degree*, e.g. 1–2 ft (30–60 cm) or to a *much smaller degree*, e.g. ¼ –½ in (approx. 1 cm). Initially, it is best to exaggerate the giving of the rein to ensure you are not fooling yourself that the horse is off the inside rein and working on the outside rein. Do this conditioning on both reins, preferably on the circle to start with, but once self-carriage is established on the circle, the rein can be given in any area of the arena.

When the horse has developed better balance, is soft in the mouth and his carriage is pleasing, you can ask for moments of self-carriage often. For example, lift the hands gently a *tiny amount* towards the horse's ears in a smooth movement of up and back again to the original hand position but such a small amount of movement is barely perceived by the onlooker. This self-carriage lifting forwards and up can either be done towards the rider's chest or towards the horse's mouth. Every horse will respond to this self-carriage enhancing and in a different way. You must try both methods to see which best suits your horse.

Once the horse is becoming established in self-carriage you will find that you can ride along holding the reins in a passive, soft way while the horse maintains the same outline and softness in the mouth, and moves in the same way, the same tempo, with the same energy, but all without any additional communication from the rider.

There was a great rider called Josef Neckermann of West Germany who was known for his ability to produce great self-carriage. It was said that he entered the Grand Prix competition arena and his horses stayed completely in self-carriage throughout the whole test. This is the ideal and, although you might not achieve this, this is the sort of good example to follow. Riding should be light and easy, fun and enjoyable for horse and rider, and a joy for the spectator.

Good rules to remember are: never push the horse forward more than you can control with your hands because it upsets rhythm and speed; never use your hands to stifle the energy or you block the horse moving forward.

Good contact builds trust, and trust builds confidence, and this makes it possible for a horse to accept submission to the rein, in other words, he accepts your authority. A horse is more powerful than you are, and when you put a bit in the horse's mouth it allows you to control that power but this control is not to be used as a braking system; the horse stops the forward momentum by engaging his hind legs, but the contact allows us to harness the energy coming through and when we contain the energy it becomes more elevated.

Self-carriage is started in droplets at the beginning of training, and it is enhanced when the horse accepts contact on both sides of the bit. When you teach him to harness his energy, you can streamline it into free expression.

Step Four: Developing Good Hands

We learn to have a good feel for the rein when we have developed an independent seat, yet 'good hands' is an elusive concept for many. For centuries riders have debated the hands of the rider and, like a musician's hands, they have to coordinate different feels but that X factor that defies analysis is also involved here. I once asked an Olympic rider, 'How do you teach the rider to have good hands, to ride with the contact but have light hands?' She did not believe you can teach it, 'You either have good hands or you don't,' she said. You are born with the gift of good riding hands.' I had to admit this is true, yet correct training does allow the rider to learn to feel good contact, to assimilate the right and wrong feelings, and to correct the horse by good use of the hands so that the training can progress.

Think about your hands, think about the stability of your position, and think about your horse and his physical and emotional needs. You cannot force a horse to do anything; if you do you will get a counter reaction, because no animal is without feelings, and bullying only gets transitory results. Bully a horse and he will have the last word, he will wait for his chance to let you know he has superior physical strength. If you show him kindness he will walk on water for you. Which attitude do you think is better? There is really no contest; kindness produces better training; any training that is not instilled with kindness is wrong, the horse's muscles will stiffen, he will resist, and the results will be bad.

If you are wise you will not attempt to control a horse by force, and this applies particularly to forcing him to come on the bit. Using force is such a sad way of training and it should never be seen in dressage riding, particularly when it is so easy to ride a horse kindly and correctly in order to bring him on to the bit. When contact is right it opens up so many possibilities, but when wrong it restricts the horse, clamps his gaits and switches him off to sensitivity.

Never mistake a light contact for letting the horse off the rein. Chucking the reins at the horse is running away from all responsibility of teaching – *it is a light rein fallacy*. Does a mother push her child across a busy road into the ongoing traffic? No. She takes her child's hand, stops at the crossing, looks right and left and if the coast is clear she leads the way across the road, and only when the child is trained to cross roads safely will she stop monitoring the process. It is a similar situation with contact. Contact is holding the horse's hand: the rein automatically becomes light once the horse is trained to accept a lighter rein contact through elevation and self-carriage.

There are two normal reactions of riders new to riding with contact: they either grasp the reins and ask for too much contact, or chuck the reins at the horse. Both problems are easy to overcome. The particular weakness must be identified and be continually checked and corrected.

A vitally important part of developing good hands is the ability to remain in balance with the horse so as not to lean on the reins to stay in the saddle, and this is furnished by a secure and independent seat. Ideally, a secure riding seat is established through lunge lessons, but this often proves unrealistic for a great many people today. The next best way for you to do this independently is to stay in walk, rising trot, and canter until a secure seat starts to develop, then, and only then, to start riding the sitting trot.

There is, however, an easier way to arrive at this point and that is to start with a horse that is not too big moving. Often a more narrow horse with less bouncy movement, such as a Thoroughbred cross, will enable you to gain a deeper seat, from which the secure and independent seat will develop. The bigger-moving warmblood is more expressive and you will need a more balanced seat to enable you to sit in harmony with the movement. However, if you already own a big-moving warmblood, yet have not developed a secure seat, and find you are struggling with improving your hands, focus on your seat. You may find a deeper-seated dressage saddle anchors you and gives you a more secure position. You may particularly like the bigger knee rolls of the modern dressage saddle that give you the flexibility to adapt your position and to place more of your weight through the knee rolls to the stirrups and then sitting up and deeper (see Chapter 2). Once you have found the key that gives you the balance required for your stage of training, and allows the powerful movement of your horse to flow through, then you will discover you are able to control your hands. Those hands, they can have a life of their own! Learn to recognize exactly what they are feeling, what signals they are giving and getting, and exactly where they should be positioned.

Sometimes circumstances are piled up against us: the rider is small, the horse is big, the rider has never established a deep seat, the horse has never been taught contact, and, in the worst scenario, the horse has an insensitive mouth through many years of being ridden incorrectly. *This* is the time to think about a way of identifying the chicken from the egg. The egg comes first, and so let's get the egg sorted, let's get the horse understanding contact.

If I have a situation such as this, or a horse that has incorrect conformation, I find ***the correct use of gadgets*** is helpful. However, ***I always advise using the de Gogue*** that is reliant on the action of the gadget itself rather than a rider's ability to use the draw reins correctly, and ***only if the rider is experienced with good hands would I consider using draw reins*** (Figures 5.12a and b and 5.13). This is because gadgets wrongly used can be disastrous and very strong on the poor horse's mouth. Be wise and be positive. Once a horse understands a designated frame helps him to remain in balance better he starts to round his back and to soften, then you will find you can sit with a deeper seat, which, in turn, leads to the development of good hands. As soon as all this falls into place, you can dispense with the gadgets and ride properly.

You may be wondering why I am talking about the seat under the section about contact, and many more details about the deep seat are contained in Chapter 2, but you will discover as you progress that the hind legs are connected to the front legs, the tail bone is connected to the poll, and the rider's seat is connected to the hands. When you feel an instant reaction to your legs applied to give forward aids – these aids bring a reaction through the horse's body and give a rounder way of going with more self-carriage – and then feel the bit in the horse's mouth soft on his tongue, at that moment you will understand completely that the way the horse moves *is* related to the way you hold the reins.

A cycle of energy flows through the horse when he moves forward and

Figures 5.12a and b   a) This overbent young gelding had been backed using draw reins by a show jumper, before his present owner bought him. We soon corrected the damage and the first stage was to teach him to go forward from the leg, and not curl back off the aids. b) Here the grey has lifted his head and neck and is moving forwards nicely and in a balanced frame. He is slightly above the bit but it is better this young horse works through the shoulder, and up and forwards.

Figure 5.13 When used correctly, draw reins are applied and loosened off so that the rider has direct contact with the snaffle rein and the correct classical head-carriage is achieved. The mare is working in four-track leg-yield.

I rarely resort to using artificial aids, the exceptions being if a rider has difficulties feeling a contact and the horse goes above the bit continuously, or if the horse has had long periods of working incorrectly, and may have had his mouth damaged by a rough rider's hands. In this case, the mare had always been ridden sympathetically, yet has a lively character and sometimes she becomes resistant. Also she had also been in and out of work owing to injuries. All these aspects combined to make it difficult for the rider to progress but draw reins helped her overcome this difficulty. If you do use draw reins I advise you to take the advice of a trainer for their correct use, and only use them for short training periods. Also, allow the horse to have breaks stretching on a long rein within the schooling sessions.

straight, working actively to the contact, and is one of the reasons why educating your hands is so fundamentally important. And, of course, having educated hands relies on the development of your seat but, in practice, these aspects cannot be separated, just as energy cannot be fixed at one point in the horse's body, since energy itself flows forwards. The question is, 'where to start?' The answer is, 'the simplest way for you to gain confidence and for the horse to improve', and so I have described below the different ways of going about training him to accept contact.

You will have already established the right bit for your horse's mouth, he will accept the bit in his mouth happily, and he will not be afraid of a contact rein. You will have taught him this by the ways explained earlier in the chapter, but if he comes to you trained but in need of improvement you may well go back and, for example, study his mouth, check he is being ridden in the right bit, and look for creative ways to give him a mouth. The solution can be as simple as giving him a long rein at the beginning of a riding session, and I am always amazed how a horse resistant to the bit will immediately relax if you give him 'space' and just drop the rein, and ride forward.

If he is rather feisty it may be wiser to keep this dropped-rein work to walk and trot on the circle, but if he is calm it can be included in walk, trot, and canter, on both the large circle and going large. Sit up, ride forward, and go on a long rein, allowing him to look for the bit himself without being continuously fiddled with. Sometimes you will discover that he has been pulled and bullied into a shape for so long by the we-have-ways-of-making-you-do-it brigade, that once you give him the tiniest bit of freedom he will think, 'wow, I like this'. You can be very surprised by the generosity of the horse, if you give to him, he will always be ready to reward you in pleasing ways.

But all horses have lively characters, and this is the aspect we love about them. They see life in black and white, and they like to keep it that way – after all it's so much easier. You will find the horse accepts contact better if you accommodate this black and white mentality, i.e. make things clear: **a contact rein is a contact rein, a long rein is a long rein and a loose rein is a loose rein**. By letting the reactionary horse off the contact rein to the long rein we have given him time to stop fighting and to come round to our way of thinking, and this often works. However, a horse who has a strong competitive spirit will still argue when you take up the contact again and you just need to persevere with, i.e. insist on, the contact rein, and give him breaks on a loose rein in free walk.

The only way to determine what sort of horse you have and the training he requires is to try different methods. The results will soon give you the answer. Do bear in mind that every horse is different, and each horse will require different things at different times of training. You must always be flexible. But, a word of warning: if every time a horse gets stroppy about accepting the contact you drop the rein and allow him a loose or long rein he will soon work out that he is on to a winning game. You will have built in a resistance to training, so be careful that you think through carefully exactly why you do anything, in what order, and how you apply the aids. Follow a consistent pattern each lesson within a training time frame.

In this chapter I have given examples of different ways to develop contact within a training session for different purposes and for different horses with different needs. It also gives pointers on what to avoid and what to aim for. I hope this will give you a thorough guide but if you are ever in doubt, drop the reins, let your horse walk on a long rein, take a deep breath, and think. Five minutes chill time should soon sort it out; you can then pick up the reins, now relaxed and refreshed, and start again.

Never get angry. Never treat the horse roughly with the reins. Remember, his mouth is as sensitive as yours, and imagine that being done to you! It is much better to relax, do something different, and come back to the problem exercise when you feel calmer. It is important to avoid letting your anger travel down the reins, it will set up a fight with the horse, and he is so much stronger than you; he will win every time, and when you have calmed down you are going to feel wretched for having lost your temper.

We are all human and we all have our moments. I refer to them as chocolate moments because it makes me laugh and reminds me that I am human and am prone to moments, weaknesses, like everybody else. The old masters counter-acted this tendency by suggesting the rider had a smoke! But since smoking is bad for your health, and it is dangerous to smoke when you ride, I suggest either going for a hack, walking on a long rein, cracking a joke with a fellow rider, or listening to music. But it is important that you recognize when you feel you are getting frustrated, and the frustration is starting to tighten the muscles in your shoulders, arms and hands. Dressage is about discipline, and when you know these moments of frustration are coming, having control over your body in positive ways means you will be able to handle them, which puts you ahead of the game. I have discussed this in more depth in Chapter 1, but felt it was important to repeat it here because I have found that many riders are more likely to get frustrated when their horses do not accept the rein because a lack of rein acceptance shows the a horse is not accepting a rider's authority.

I expect you are like me, that you rarely feel angry with a horse but I warn you that it will occur even with the most patient rider, and I ask that you take this into account when you consider developing a rider's hands. The hands are influenced by the brain and the emotions and this will be reflected in the way a rider takes up the contact.

6 EASY SIDEWAYS

THREE THINGS COVER everything the horse needs to do dressage: to go forwards, to stop, and to go sideways. Lateral work can be neglected by dressage riders at the lower levels, but this is a shame because it provides so many benefits, it strengthens the horse's muscular system, supples and straightens in a unique way. Dressage would be limited without lateral work. Once you get going with sideways riding you will soon see improvements, and don't be daunted by it because it is easy when you know the techniques of the exercises.

Terminology can be confusing, there are, for example: 30 per cent angles, coordinating inside and outside aids in different places and to different intensities, hands to the inside, hands to the outside, indirect rein, open rein, but once understood there really is no problem. Just take it one step at a time giving yourself time for the different aids to become second nature, and the best way to achieve this is to work in walk to allow everything (the aids, the causes and effects) to sink into your subconscious mind and the skills to come gradually. A trainer, or a knowledgeable friend watching from the ground, helps speed up progress. Do not worry about these exercises, just start with easy ones like leg-yielding, and do the more difficult exercises when you feel confident, and the horse is ready.

Using walk gives you time to figure out the aids and also gives the horse time to step through the movements more easily. If he has never performed this work before, certain aspects, such as the crossing of his legs, can upset him, but if he is walking the exercise he will relax. Walk gives his brain time to check his reactions to your aids, and he should show a willingness to do well. If you reward him for trying, he will start to enjoy it.

So, keep new exercises in walk until collected trot has begun, although some leg-yielding exercises are more easily ridden in working trot. Allow the particular abilities of each horse to dictate which gait to use, for example, some have a neat trot and can slip into trot lateral work before they can do collected trot. But with big-moving horses it is safer to wait until collection is established.

As we have discussed, horses can be like naughty school boys, they love to be mischievous, especially highly strung horses. This type can use the spring of the trot to avoid doing the work properly, or by evading stepping forward fluidly and the trot will become bunched up. You should, therefore, wait for the horse to tell you if he is ready to progress to trot and if he is not ready, revert to walk returning to trot at a later date. If things go pear-shaped (because we do not live in a perfect world) do not panic, refresh the gaits with brisk working trot, or canter to trot transitions, and these exercises alone often put problems right. Remember that horses are more forgiving than you imagine; if you make a mistake, put things right and move on.

Suppling the Shoulders

When the shoulders are suppled it helps straighten the horse and lets the energy flow through from the hindquarters to the forehand. All exercises for suppling the shoulders derive from the shoulder-in exercise developed by the French classical school rider, de la Guérinière, who said, 'I regard the shoulder-in as an indispensable aid in achieving flexibility of the shoulders and the ability to cross the legs easily. A perfection which all horses must have if they are to be called well-formed and well trained.' *Ecole de Cavalerie*, 1733

The shoulder-in is invaluable for the horse, it is impossible to ride good dressage without it. But I reiterate: start slowly and always in walk; do not proceed to trot until the exercise is well learnt, and leave some shoulder-suppling exercises until collected trot is started. You will find more details on this in the Easy Sideways gait table (see page 223) for riding these exercises.

When you start trot lateral work begin in rising trot. Avoid sitting trot until:

1. The horse's back is strong enough to bear the weight of the rider in sitting trot.

2. You are sure the diagonals in the trot are working through equally from the hindquarters to the front of the horse so that each diagonal is of the same length, stepping up and forwards in throughness equally.

3. Your seat is alive (supple with the horse's movement), and you are sure you are not restricting the free forward movement of the trot if you ride in sitting trot.

Rising trot offers the rider many training advantages such as straightening the horse by making the diagonalization of the trot steps equal without any resistances coming through your back, giving the horse greater freedom of expression and promoting the elegance and fluidity of movement. For reasons such as these some Grand Prix riders use rising trot shoulder-in as a warm-up exercise. Some riders say they prefer riding sitting trot, but it is not always easier for the horse, especially if the rider's seat is not absorbing the energy. Keep an open mind, consider the best approach for your horse and be guided by this. Combine it with the proven methods that are outlined in this book.

Do not overdo any lateral exercise. For example, do not go beyond half the length of the arena in shoulder-in until the horse is really strong and supple, and start every new exercise with just a few steps on each rein. Ride straight work for longer than lateral work; never exceed the proportion of two thirds straight work to one third lateral work. Keep it simple for yourself and your horse and remember the golden rule: revert to basic exercises if an exercise does not progress smoothly.

You can, however, solve many problems simply by riding your horse in walk on a loose rein giving you both a breather, a moment to chill out, a time when inspiration can come. If an answer does not present itself immediately, do not punish yourself, it might not have been meant to happen that day, perhaps it will come another day. If you adopt this calm approach to problem solving you will sail ahead and confidence will grow. It is a wonderful feeling when you and your horse work out situations together. If the results of your thoughts match the feelings you experience when you ride, you will work logically through problematical riding situations.

Lateral work has defined rules that help you to think through situations, and make it easier to identify causes and effects. Points to consider are:

- Have you asked a horse to perform a new exercise before he is ready?
- Are you pulling on the inside rein and blocking the inside shoulder and the engagement of the inside leg?
- Is the outside contact too strong and stopping inside bend?
- Does the horse have enough room to step off the track so that he is not scrunching his quarters along the wall of the arena? (Big horses and horses with long backs need more room to do shoulder-in exercises. They get put off if they bang their hind legs on the walls of the school and will curl up in a banana shape because they are nervous of hurting themselves).
- Is the horse finding it easy? Is he willing to try to respond to your requests, or is he resisting?

If an exercise puts you off balance, or you are pulling or shoving, you could either be taking the wrong approach or the horse is not ready for the exercise. Take a break and, while riding around, think through the aids for the exercise and think through the horse's reactions, and then try again with the information you have gleaned. If the results are still not good, try another exercise, one that is more basic or that your horse knows already, and reward him when he responds well to the easier work. You can return to the problem exercise another day, which could be the next day or months away depending on your horse. Stay sensitive to his needs and to his physical development and only return to the exercise when he is ready.

Working with a trainer makes it easier for you to identify problems, but a friend or horsy colleague can help too. Ask someone to video you riding so that you can study it later, or ask a competent rider to watch you and make constructive comments. To get the most from help on the ground, direct the helper to stand in the most advantageous place for a particular exercise (for shoulder-in, for example, this would be at the end of the long side of the arena so the angle and bend can be seen) and give her specific points you want her to look for.

Instruction from a trainer combined with help from a friend can kick-start your progress, but watching, and receiving advice from, an experienced dressage rider is priceless. You learn from other riders while teaching yourself and being aware of what you are aiming for. This three-pronged approach boosts your understanding and mistakes can be avoided, and such open-minded training helps your relationship with your horse. Sometimes all it takes to solve a problem is a good night's sleep; when you wake the answer comes to you because your brain has figured it out while you were dreaming sweet dreams.

Lateral work moves *forward and sideways* (crabs move sideways and sideways) follow this rule and you will be doing really well. A golden rule to ensure you prevent mistakes is to do just a few quality steps each session and no more. Build on these few steps gradually until you can string them together.

Lateral work teaches the rider to ride every side of the horse. It seems an obvious statement to make, and yet all riders have a tendency to focus on the front and back of the horse, instead of taking into account the fact that the horse has: a front, a back, a left side, and a right side. Never fail to see the wood for the trees because you restrict your riding and the potential of the horse, but if you ride lateral exercises logically and well, your abilities will open up. The beauty of the horse's gaits will also improve as his shoulders become supple and allow the energy through to the bit.

Dressage is shoulders in front of the hindquarters. This is a continental expression meaning that unless the horse goes *straight* the energy cannot flow through to maximize the beauty of the gaits. Shoulder-in exercises promote the ability to position the shoulders in front of the quarters in a unique way. Normally leg-yielding exercises are taught to start with. Initial lateral training can begin early, after six months to a year, or even sooner if you are experienced and keep the horse's needs in mind. Follow the rules of each exercise carefully, do not rush the horse and be sympathetic and understanding. If a horse gets hot when learning a new exercise teach it one day, give him several days rest, giving him time to mull it over in his mind, and return to the new exercise. You will find he will now be happy about the work, he will think he is very clever to have figured it out, and he will be happy to oblige you. If you have a horse who has the temperament for, and just loves, new work, teach him a new exercise and then practise it daily, but still only do a few steps at a time, building on this gradually, as explained above.

When different lateral exercises are bedded in, you can combine different ones together to get different effects. For example, using travers on the hollow side, adding in a small 10 m circle halfway along the arena, then riding shoulder-in with less inside bend helps supple the muscles of the diagonal on the hollow side, and even the horse's acceptance of the bit.

Adapt your riding regime to suit your horse. New exercises use muscles in a way the horse has not experienced before and if you do not allow time for soreness to heal he may become stiff and resistant. Encourage your horse to produce good quality work that is easy for him. It normally takes a year to progress to a well-ridden three-track shoulder-in, but it does depend on the knowledge of the rider and the talents of the horse.

Practise with care and you will find horses love learning lateral work. It will make him straighter, his gaits will show more spring, he will accept the contact better, and he will be easier to ride; there are so many benefits to lateral work. Riding a horse with supple shoulders is like driving a car with power steering, the going is lighter, smoother, and more fun.

EXERCISES FOR SUPPLING THE SHOULDERS

The first aim of lateral exercises is to communicate to the horse that the forward/sideways leg is different from the forward/straight leg. The best way to do this is to teach him new exercises as you would teach a child to read and write: the teacher begins with simple words, spells out each letter clearly, and then the pupil joins them together; she starts writing on lined paper and progresses to unlined, but is not rushed through the learning stages. Often the teacher will go back and check the understanding is consolidated, never expecting a child to write essays before she can do simple words such as **cat** or **dog**, for example. The same rule applies to teaching horses. The acronym KISS (keep it sweet and simple) applies to teaching dressage, and especially to new lateral-work exercises. Dressage exercises for suppling the shoulders are listed below.

1. Leg-yield/turn on the forehand on the circle.

2. Turn on the forehand.
3. Leg-yield parallel to the track.
4. Leg-yield/shoulder-in
5. Shoulder-fore
6. Shoulder-in
7. Position renvers to position shoulder-in
8. Renvers.

Leg-yield/turn on the forehand on the circle

This exercise combines asking the horse to move over from the open and indirect rein aids with the effects of the horse reacting to you positioning yourself in the direction of the new movement by sitting square to axis in relation to that direction and the horse reacting to these new seat aids through his centre of gravity. He is primed to keep his balance through the directional and seat changes and learns to anticipate the changes. The aids are synchronized and with intelligent riding can indicate to the horse that he is being asked for this type of lateral work rather than work on straight lines.

This exercise also teaches a horse to move over from the outside leg behind the girth (the leg position can be just 3 in [7.5 cm] or up to 1 ft [30 cm] behind the girth to start with) and leads on to the next lateral movement: reversed shoulder-in along the long side.

This turn on the forehand on the circle is a leg-yield exercise that exaggerates leg-yield and uses it as a form of neck bend/leg-yield, so that even the stiffest horse, or the slowest to learn new exercises, reacts quickly to this new training. It is also extremely easy for riders new to lateral work to do within a few minutes of being taught the exercise.

It is performed in walk on a small circle for a short period of time (i.e. no more than two minutes on each rein). It is a good exercise to start off lateral work because it introduces the horse to the rider sitting square to axis for sideways work, and initiates the horse's understanding of the sideways leg. Once he is familiar with, and well established in, other basic lateral work it is normal to stop this exercise, but it can be useful when ridden on a 20 m circle in trot if, for example, a horse tends to grab one rein, or stiffens through the body on one side to the bit. Do not overdo this exercise and as soon as the horse has derived benefit from the exercise, ride him forward in classical exercises.

It is easy to ride, because the horse is put in a position that makes it natural for him to step sideways from the leg.

How to ride leg-yield/turn on the forehand on the circle
Bring the horse to halt and position him in the opposite direction to which he is about to move, e.g., in this case, you are going to position him to the left and move him to the right. Ask for left bend, the amount of which depends on your horse, but you can exaggerate it, especially for a stiff horse, by opening the inside rein wide. The inside left rein is open, and the outside right rein, the indirect rein, is positioned close to the neck at the withers. Make sure you keep your thumb up on this outside rein and a steady connection with the bit because this is the outside contact, which helps to teach a horse the acceptance of a steady outside contact rein. Do not drop the inside rein or lean the weight of your arm on it; think of it as an opportunity to open a door, i.e. teach the open rein.

The exercise introduces sitting square to axis to the horse in an easy way. You must remember to keep your shoulders and hips parallel to those of the horse. He is positioned differently from when moving on straight lines and your shoulders and hips must mirror those of the horse when you ask him to bend. It should happen in a smooth, flowing action so that the horse will understand sitting square to axis as an aid. It makes him lighter to the hand aids because it induces better acceptance of the outside rein and a softer feel on the inside rein.

Put your inside (left) knee into the saddle roll and take your inside (left) lower leg away from the horse's side (this can be a little or a lot depending on the horse's sensitivity). Now position your leg 2–6 in (5–15 cm) behind the girth making sure you do not drag your leg back or keep your leg pressed on giving an unwanted aid. Most horses prefer 6 in (15 cm) at least so that the forward/sideways aid is distinct from the forward leg aid. Then put the leg on quietly and use the heel to press into the horse's side gently in a tapping motion. Once he takes a step sideways, release the leg aid, and reapply it for each step sideways you want the horse to make. Ensure that the outside leg is held away from the outside of the horse, so that you are not blocking him from moving

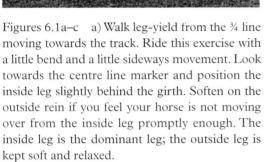

Figures 6.1a–c a) Walk leg-yield from the ¾ line moving towards the track. Ride this exercise with a little bend and a little sideways movement. Look towards the centre line marker and position the inside leg slightly behind the girth. Soften on the outside rein if you feel your horse is not moving over from the inside leg promptly enough. The inside leg is the dominant leg; the outside leg is kept soft and relaxed.

b) and c) Walk leg-yielding on the circle. This is similar to leg-yielding back to the track as shown in the previous photograph except that you are positioned for the line of the circle and you can ask for more head and neck bend and more sideways stepping. You can increase the amount of inside bend and bring the inside leg further back if your horse is stiff. Ride it with little bend first to see how the horse reacts. Do not overdo the amount of time you spend riding this exercise, a maximum of five minutes on each rein will suffice, and often less time is enough to soften the horse to the aids, and only increase the inside bend if the horse stiffens against the leg aids. For example, little bend, little sideways, the rider in the photograph is looking towards the centre line marker and has the inside leg slightly behind the girth. Soften on the outside rein if you feel your horse is not moving over from the inside leg promptly enough. The inside leg is the dominant leg; the outside leg is kept soft and relaxed.

sideways from the inside leg, and that you are sitting correctly when you ask for the bend; make sure your body mirrors the bend of the horse, i.e. bring your outside shoulder and hip forward, and inside shoulder and hip back.

The horse will be stepping sideways on a small circle (Figures 6.1a–c). Stop the exercise after 2–5 strides and pat the horse. Repeat the exercise, perform it on the other rein, and finish it on the rein on which he finds the exercise easier. Give him a big pat and return to simple forward-and-straight work.

Turn on the forehand

Use the turn on the forehand with discretion; it is a useful training exercise but is not a movement required in dressage tests. It is, however, the exercise that will teach a horse to move correctly away from a gate when you need to open one when out hacking. The turn on the forehand is also helpful if a horse is sensitive to the leg or hesitant about learning other lateral work.

How to ride turn on the forehand

Stand the horse square one horse's length inside the track on the long side of the school. A normal turn on the forehand is always ridden from the halt. This distinguishes it from the modern exercise of turn on the forehand on the move, on the circle (see pages 205–206). If working on the left rein, position the horse slightly to the left, i.e. with left inside bend, position the inside (left) leg slightly behind the girth 2–4 in (5–10 cm) and nudge the horse sideways. You may find you need to give and take on the outside rein if he moves over too quickly. Ask for the side stepping slowly. Perform this exercise a few times on each rein.

As with the turn on the forehand on the circle, horses find this exercise easy. The horse's quarters move around his forehand (the opposite to a pirouette where the forehand is moved around his quarters – a collecting exercise). Be careful not to overdo these turn-on-the-forehand exercises because they put the horse on the forehand and he may show an artificial over-collection by coming into a form of collection that evades the energy coming through his body to the bit. For example, some horses bunch themselves up when they get stressed or over-excited and this false collection is not what is required in dressage work because calmness is paramount to the horse using his body well and to his ability to receive instructions from the rider. If a horse has a tendency to artificial collection through over-excitement, the turn-on-the-forehand exercises stretch the muscles of the topline and counteract the inclination to bunch up. Although over-use of the turn on the forehand can place a horse on his forehand more, this is a drawback that can be accepted because the use of *slightly* longer periods of turn on the forehand, turn on the forehand on the circle and leg-yield exercises can help the training of the horse who cannot accept dressage training without displaying anxiety or tension, unlike his calmer counterpart. Such is the power of lateral work to build harmony between horse and rider.

Leg-yield parallel to the track

This is an easy exercise to teach the horse sideways movement, but is less useful once the horse understands the more established exercise of leg-yield/shoulder-in and shoulder-in, for example. Once this stage is reached I stop using it, unless for specific purposes with other lateral work. For example, combined with half-pass it helps improve inside bend. Also, when it is combined with a few steps of shoulder-in along a straight line, it keeps the horse moving from one exercise to another, and this keeps him sharp off the aids.

How to ride leg-yield parallel to the track

Ride down the long side of the arena, through the first corner of the short side, keep riding past the centre line and turn up the ¾ line. Make sure you make a clean turn, do not pull on the inside rein to turn the horse. Once the horse is on a straight line keep travelling at the same rhythm, and then bend him slightly to the inside with an open inside rein, opening to about ½–1 in (1–2.5 cm), and position the outside rein close to the neck. Position the inside leg about 1–2 in (2.5–5 cm) behind the girth and keep the outside leg relaxed; this ensures that you do not block the horse by jamming the outside leg on. Squeeze gently with the inside leg so that the horse steps very slightly sideways. There is no rush for him to return to the track, just make sure he goes forward steadily, and just a *very little* sideways so that he gradually returns to the track.

Tips on sitting square to axis

As soon as you have turned up the ¾ line, look towards the half marker of C or A, depending on from which direction you approach it, positioning the shoulders and seat towards it *very slightly.* When the horse returns to the long side of the arena reposition your upper body for riding along the straight line.

LEG-YIELD EXERCISES
Leg-yield/shoulder-in and reversed leg-yield/shoulder-in

The leg-yield/shoulder-in exercises look exactly like shoulder-in and, also like shoulder-in, the horse looks in the opposite direction to the direction of the movement, but these exercises differ in two respects.

1. They can be ridden with more angle (up to a maximum of 45 degrees).
2. There is no bend through the body.

These exercises can be ridden along the track, on the circle, through the corner, or along the ¼ or ¾ lines. They are easier for the horse to perform and the rider to ride and are good exercises for starting lateral work. They can be ridden as **leg-yield/shoulder-in** (Figure 6.2) or taken along the walls of the arena so that the horse has his head facing the barrier of the wall (this helps to hold him on the line of movement) when the exercise becomes **reversed leg-yield/shoulder-in**, and it also prepares the horse for travers (Figure 6.3).

Riding leg-yield/shoulder-in

Some horses find it easier to do these exercises on corners or circles because they feel there is more room to move and they are better prepared for inside bend if you prepare for a little more bend as you approach the corner. If you have plenty of inside bend as you ride towards a corner, the exercise can evolve into a circle once the horse has the gist of the exercise. Some horses respond well to the modern lateral-work aids even though they are the opposite of the classical aids because they require suppleness and bend through accurate riding, whereas the modern leg-yield exercises actually make use of the horse's stiffness and supple him by preparing him in a constructive way. Also you can develop competence, learn to understand angles and amounts of flexion/bend and where and how to use the different lateral work without causing a major problem with shoulder-in work,

Figure 6.2 (*above left*) Trot leg-yield/shoulder-in. This movement looks like shoulder-in but the horse is positioned at a maximum of a 45 degree angle to the track and works on four tracks whereas the shoulder-in is ridden at the lesser angle of 30 degrees and goes on three-tracks. The inside leg is used behind the girth instead of on the girth as for shoulder-in, and more inside bend can be asked for, depending on the needs of the horse.

Here we see the mare moving at a good angle in a nice bend.

Figure 6.3 (*above right*) Walk reversed leg-yield/shoulder-in. This exercise uses exactly the same aids as for leg-yield/shoulder-in but they are reversed and the horse is ridden down the track with the head facing the barrier.

when if it is not ridden correctly, you can disconnect the horse from the outside rein, over-bend the side of the horse's body and plonk the horse on the inside rein too much, causing the benefits of lateral work to be negated. But by learning through exercises that resemble true classical lateral exercises but without body bend (making them leg-yield exercises) you overcome all the potential hazards and build up a repertoire of riding skills that develop your ability to identify whether a horse performs a classical lateral movement incorrectly. Eventually you will have suppled your horse beyond the norm and this will be reflected in his gaits being of a higher standard than would have been achieved without this exercise.

However, you still need to teach inside leg to outside rein, and shoulder-in teaches this well. If you opt for the modern approach, therefore, do check that you do not overdo it, and always return to the classical way of riding.

To achieve more bend through the front of the horse to start suppling him in preparation for improved bend through the body bring yourself round a little to sit square to axis, hold your inside leg *very softly* against the horse's side, and wait for the horse to look for your leg, i.e. you apply your leg more positively around his side and give him a more positive cuddle feel through this leg. Providing this is ridden correctly, it should begin to feel like the horse's body comes to meet the inside of your boot (at about the top of the boot). Of course, this depends on the length of your legs, and the depth of the horse's barrel, but generally this is about the point at which you should feel the movement. Once you feel this coming of the horse to your leg, that is the moment to apply the inside leg, and you will feel the horse stepping sideways in leg-yield/shoulder-in but with more bend through his head and neck. Allow the movement for just a few steps, and then go straight, prolonging the length of the exercise as the horse improves.

N.B: the inside leg is kept on the girth or a little forward of the girth, and is good preparation for shoulder-in since the inside leg is not positioned behind the girth. When the leg is positioned thus, the movement is a leg-yield because the horse moves away from your inside leg and the greater degree of bend gives a type of neck-bend/leg-yield effect that puts the horse into the movement. The leg applied behind the girth pushing the quarters away helps the bend to be increased more if you feel this is beneficial and does not upset the horse's balance. These actions instigate increased stretching of the muscles throughout the horse's body and the exaggerated crossing over of his front and hind legs, and this maximizes the stretching element of this exercise. When performed in walk the horse can be asked for the maximum stretch he can cope with but in trot the angles, neck bend and crossing of the limbs should be lessened to approximate those of the classical shoulder-in exercise. However, once the horse is comfortable with this work in both walk and trot, more stretching can be asked for. I do, nevertheless, advise that you never ask the horse to stretch for any longer than five minutes and always give the horse periods of walk on a long rein before continuing the work in order to avoid muscle tension or any contusion of the horse's musculature.

The further forward the inside leg is positioned, the closer it resembles shoulder-in. The classical shoulder-in inside leg position is slightly forward of the girth in the area of the first rib because that is where the bend comes from.

It is worth noting that if you position your inside leg too far back you take away true bend. Bend in these leg-yield exercises is shown through the head and neck only, which explains why it can be ridden with greater bend.

Teach leg-yield/shoulder-in across the diagonal by starting the reversed leg-yield exercise but, instead of going down the track, give one or two half-halts on the inside rein to lead the horse across the diagonal line. Some horses prefer to come along the centre line to X, and leg-yield from X to one of the quarter markers: F, H, K or M, especially those new to the exercise, because the space seems more inviting to their eyes and they have a natural inclination to want to return to the track. Horses that benefit from leg-yield across the diagonal tend to be eager and have a powerful bouncy stride. This is not a classical exercise but is useful for checking that the horse is on the aids and, at the same time, prompting his forward momentum, because it can be ridden in a strong working trot. Do not use this movement excessively. Start it in walk to give a horse time to understand it, but move into trot as soon as possible. It really is a trot sideways movement.

Riding reversed leg-yield/shoulder-in

It is ridden the same way as explained in the leg-yield/turn-on-the-forehand movement. In all shoulder-ins and leg-yield/shoulder-ins you are looking for responses to the inside leg, and hold a steady consistent outside rein with an open inside rein and a soft outside leg.

In order to **sit square to axis** in this exercise, make sure your shoulder and hip positioning mirrors that of the horse as explained in the other exercises.

Shoulder-fore and shoulder-in

All shoulder-in work is really very simple: the horse's shoulders are moved off the track! My mother was a complete amateur when it came to dressage but when she watched my first lessons in shoulder-in she explained to me, 'No dumb-bell, shoulder-in is easy, *it is shoulders in off the track*.' I got the message regarding this simple truth quickly, and soon found riding shoulder-in easy.

The shoulders follow different lines from those the quarters follow because the horse is positioned at a 30 degree angle in three-track shoulder-in and it is this version of shoulder-in on which you should focus your understanding. Four-track shoulder-in is reserved for High School work and is rarely seen nowadays, even in Grand Prix dressage. The following steps show how the horse moves in three-track shoulder in.

- The inside foreleg follows a line *inside* the inside line of the track.
- The outside foreleg and inside hind leg follow the same line *on* the inside line of the track or approximately on the *central* part of the track.
- The outside hind leg moves *on a separate line* to the inside hind leg and outside foreleg and is positioned to the outside of the track.

To ride the three-track shoulder-in requires rider skill and suppleness of the horse. For these reasons and to prevent the horse stepping out of the correct shoulder-in position thus evading the benefits of the exercise and to supple him up gradually to prepare him for correct shoulder-in, experienced riders tend to train towards it through **position shoulder-in** and then progressing towards **shoulder-fore**. Position shoulder-in has the smallest angle; shoulder-fore has a slightly greater angle, and then comes three-track shoulder-in. The difference between these positions and leg-yielding is that the angles are less than the leg-yielding angle because they are never greater than the horse can maintain with a uniform bend from head to tail. Hence the reason why leg yielding is so helpful to start suppling the shoulders and get the horse ready for the real shoulder-in.

I will explain how to ride shoulder-fore in detail below and the same aids apply to position shoulder-in (the position with a lesser angle than shoulder fore) but they are *distinctly* finer aids, indeed they are barely perceptible except to an experienced eye. In fact, they are easier to ride because they are such fine aids and you can think of the move as forwards sideways with more bend. If you are in any doubt about how to ride position shoulder-in, ride shoulder-fore and the practical experience of riding this movement will give you the confidence to progress to this work.

These shoulder-in exercises are so beneficial to improving the engagement of the horse's hindquarters, the lightening of his forehand and his acceptance of the bit that I would really encourage you to persevere with the exercises. A mirror placed at the end of the arena helps you to develop an eye for the correctness of the angles you are riding. Alternatively ask a friend to stand at the end of the arena and to inform you about what is happening. Being *exact* about this work and thinking in a *precise* way will automatically build up your expertise in this lateral work. It is easy once you get going and so keep practising until you can ride excellent position shoulder-in, shoulder-fore and shoulder-in. This work is so fundamental to good dressage work that you will have made a wise investment in your training.

Another way of understanding these positions is to understand that the track is like a railway track, i.e. there are two lines and a space between. The outside line should never be crossed, the track is used, and the inside line is used, or crossed over, so that the shoulders travel at an angle to the rest of the horse's body. When riding lateral work on a circle, imagine a child's train set with the tracks going in straight lines to circles. This may help you understand riding lateral work on the circle, but below I explain how to look for the line of the angle to make it easy.

How to ride shoulder-fore
The best way to start shoulder-fore is to ride the bend, i.e. to come along the long side of the arena, ask for inside bend with your inside leg a little forward, and position the bend with both reins a little to the inside. The outside rein moves inwards approximately 4–6 in (10–15 cm) i.e. the width of both hands, and stays still keeping a consistent steady contact while the inside rein is held open to about 1–2 in (2.5–5 cm). Look across the arena to the opposite corner

in the direction in which you are travelling and/or the opposite quarter marker nearest this corner. Do not ask for too much sideways movement, do not even think sideways but just think going forward with a little more bend. This exercise will progress into the proper shoulder-fore movement.

Sit square to axis and look across the arena as explained above, this will weight the inside seat bone a little. Check that your body is not tipping to the inside and that your seat is parallel to the horse's shoulders. Let the inside leg hang down in a relaxed way so that it is positioned under your hip and seat bone. Do not clamp on to the horse's side with your leg but use it in a natural way. Remember to keep the outside leg snowflake soft. Both hands come a little to the inside as the rider begins the movement and remain still but if the horse stiffens you can soften the inside rein a little to soften his acceptance of the bit. Also, softening the inside rein and then giving the rein so that the horse is only on the outside contact is good for conditioning the horse for self-carriage.

This sequence of photographs (Figures 6.4a–d) shows how easily you can practise the different positions and angles of shoulder-fore, shoulder-in and leg-yield/shoulder-in, and once the basic leg-yields are taught it is useful to do them as separate exercises to supple the horse in different ways. For example, a leg-yield/shoulder-in with plenty of angle helps ease stiffness in a horse who is particularly resistant in a training session. A few minutes in this work followed by correct shoulder-in exercises irons out the stiffness, gives suppleness through the leg-yielding and greater obedience, followed by better acceptance of the bit through shoulder-in.

Figures 6.4a–d   a) Riding shoulder-in by asking for increased bend with the inside leg on the girth while riding through the corner and at the same time looking slightly to the opposite corner, and showing shoulder-fore (i.e. the inside front leg is on the inside line of the track. b) Walk three-track shoulder-in with very slightly more position to allow for the mare's length of body. c) The horse has moved into leg-yield stepping the outside foreleg just a little too much over the inside line of the track. d) A definite leg-yield: the horse has stepped over too much and come out of shoulder-in position. If the rider had softened on the outside rein and put on more inside leg for a few strides this would have been corrected.

You have until Elementary level before shoulder-in is required in competition, and learning the different correct angles for the different exercises early helps fine-tune your feel for them.

Figures 6.5a and b   Another way to teach the shoulder-in is to ride it around a corner with plenty of bend around a relaxed inside leg.

Three-track shoulder-in

The other exercises are so comprehensive that by the time you start shoulder-in you will find it easy. You are already familiar with the aids because you have ridden reversed shoulder-in, position shoulder-in, shoulder-fore, and shoulder-in around the corner, and so this new work should now present no problems (Figures 6.5a and b).

How to ride three-track shoulder-in

Sit as if in shoulder-fore but ask for a little more angle (30 degrees) and slightly more inside bend, but be careful not to overdo this. To keep the angle consistent at 30 degrees, look across the diagonal line – this is the normal way of riding shoulder-in. But some horses work better if you look towards the opposite corner rather than the quarter marker if they have a tendency to step out of the correct three tracks, and/or tend to evade the 30 degree angle and the correct bend. You have to work out which way suits your horse.

Ensure that the horse comes into, moves along, and moves out of, the shoulder-in with the same rhythm of the gait you are using. Once this is firmly established, you can alter the tempo to keep the horse lively off the aids. Other exercises include: a few steps of shoulder-in to medium trot moving across the diagonal line; a few steps of shoulder-in to half-pass; riding half the arena in shoulder-in to a small circle and travers; or using more angle and bend for a leg-yield/shoulder-in to a true classical shoulder-in.

A mirror placed at the end of the arena is a helpful aid; you can see if the angle and bend are absolutely correct, otherwise you have to rely on an assistant on the ground to check for you. Getting the feel of the correct angle can only be achieved by practising correctly so that you get the feel built into your seat and know precisely when the horse is going wrong, and can correct it.

Make sure the horse has enough room to move, horses get upset if they bang their hind legs on a wall of the arena, and can curl away from the movement.

Position renvers to shoulder-fore

This exercise combines shoulder-fore with a slight renvers positioning rather than a full renvers exercise. This makes it suitable for horses already familiar with shoulder-fore work and it is really beneficial for softening the horse on the contact. It is best started on the circle. The exercise is ridden from one long side to the other. Ride the horse in a slight angled shoulder-fore around the short side of the arena, come round, and after travelling 6 or 7 strides across the school, straighten the horse and then put him in position renvers for a few steps. Straighten him again before reaching the track, go forward for a few strides and return to a few steps of shoulder-fore. This exercise supples the poll and keeps the horse sweet to the leg (Figure 6.6).

When you want more softness in the mouth or poll, or if you want the horse to come softer off the leg, do this exercise a few times on each rein as you ride around the arena. The exercise can be ridden on the simple shape described above, when it becomes a specific exercise, and once it is

understood it can also be used in small doses with your general riding. Be careful not to overdo it, just a few steps of position renvers to shoulder-fore or position shoulder-in, for example. This exercise can also be ridden as simply positions through the head and neck, i.e. positions coming just from the bend in the poll rather than the full movement. You can alter the exercise to suit the needs of the horse. Often *less is better* and doing less of an exercise can bring good results. The general rule is, therefore, if you get the required result by asking for less of this exercise, so much the better, but the only way to know how much of this work is needed is to try it in different ways with your horse and see what suits him best.

Figure 6.6   Position renvers is an exercise good for suppling the poll.

How to ride position renvers to shoulder-fore
Coming into the movement, sit lightly on the outside seat bone and ask for bend around the outside leg; the outside has now become the inside. With lateral work the bend is always to the inside. This rule makes it easy to remember the inside aids. The inside leg (previously the outside leg) asking for the bend is kept very soft and applied just behind the girth to hold the quarters to the movement. The exercise is asking for positioning through the poll slightly towards the bend. A typical example is the half-pass when the horse moves in a half-pass loop back to the track. What was the rider's inside leg has now, strictly speaking, become the outside leg and because the horse is looking and bending towards the direction in which he is moving, the rider's leg on the side of the bend now becomes the inside leg despite the fact that it faces the outside of the arena.

The hands are held close together, both close to the withers to keep hand movements to a minimum, although they can be held slightly away from the withers for those horses who prefer the hands held slightly wider apart. Both legs are kept soft, barely touching the horse's sides, and the movement is ridden from soft hands asking for position through the head and neck of the horse.

Renvers (quarters out)

Renvers, or quarters out, is ridden at a 30 degree angle like shoulder-in but the horse is looking in the direction of the movement. A good way to start is to ride in shoulder-in with just a little bend, to reposition the horse by the outside leg becoming the inside leg and asking for bend, and riding as explained above.

TIPS FOR RIDING LATERAL WORK

Riders often get confused by these lateral aids but to overcome any confusion remember these two rules.

1. In dressage no matter what rein you are working on, the **inside** is the side facing the **inside of the arena** and the **outside** is the side facing the **outside of the arena**.

2. **In lateral work this can differ**. With all travers, renvers and half-pass exercises the inside is the side of the bend in the horse's body. The horse moves forwards and sideways towards the direction in which he is moving and this direction in which he is moving is always referred to as the inside.

Remember to follow the process of teaching lateral work in simple steps as explained before and take it steadily a few steps at a time in each training session.

It is easier to begin riding this lateral work using only the inside leg otherwise you tend to jam on the outside leg and stop the sideways movement, which can be very confusing for the horse. Over a period of six months to a year the aids become so well coordinated, and the horse so finely tuned to you sitting square to axis for the lateral work that the outside leg can be brought into play. In all leg-yielding and shoulder-in exercises the outside leg is applied snowflake soft unless the horse moves too fast off the inside leg, in which case it can be used more firmly to re-establish the rhythm. Also when you sit square to axis your seat bones are engaged to the correct amount and this positions you to use the correct degree of inside and outside leg.

Lateral work does require an enormous amount of body coordination, and it is better that you accept this and take things slowly, not putting yourself under stress to plough through the exercises too quickly. Also, you will have learnt the inside leg application from the shoulder-in work, and that of the outside leg through riding reversed shoulder-in, and these skills give you an added dimension to other dressage work, such as riding inside leg to outside rein. All your dressage riding will improve and experience will make teaching horses the exercises so much easier (Figure 6.7).

Figure 6.7   The beginnings of shoulder-in with a horse who had been backed just a few months. I call this a baby shoulder-in because the horse is just starting the exercise and it is ridden in the simplest, easiest way, asking only as much as the horse can give generously and without resistance. The movement lies between leg-yield and shoulder-in, and shows good inside bend. Some horses worry about knocking themselves on the arena fencing and so doing this exercise along the centre line rather than the track can help overcome this fear. Also, the rider can position the horse to a lesser, or greater, angle easily.

This rider taught lateral work to her established mare, which enabled her to teach her young horse quickly and easily. In fact, this was only the third time it had been performed with this horse.

It is best to stick to walk lateral work when you first start a new exercise and avoid doing trot lateral work other than leg-yields until collected trot is started.

GAIT TABLE FOR SHOULDER-SUPPLING EXERCISES

LATERAL WORK	WALK	TROT	CANTER
Leg-yield/Turn on the forehand on the circle	Yes, but normally done from halt to walk.	Sometimes, but on the 20 m circle rather than the 10 m circle.	No
Turn on the forehand	Halt to stepping over and not moving forwards.	No	No
Leg-yield parallel to the track	Yes, a little.	Yes, including working trot.	Preferably no, it puts too much strain on horse's limbs.
Leg-yield/ shoulder-in and reversed leg-yield/ shoulder-in	Yes, to introduce the exercise and for suppling and warming up stiff horses, and those who need bringing onto the aids.	Yes, working and collected trot.	No, there are trainers that use it but I find it puts too much strain on the horse's limbs.
Shoulder-fore	Yes, especially for the first stages of teaching the movement.	Yes. This movement is mainly ridden in trot, however, if you have a big moving horse defer progressing to trot until collected trot is established. Also, horses with big springy steps can use the suspension in the trot to evade performing the movement well, and this negates the benefits of shoulder-in, so for these types add plenty of walk shoulder-fore alongside trotting.	Canter – yes, but be careful, and look at the notes below. Only advanced riders, or competent students with knowledgeable trainers, should use canter, but if it is ridden correctly it can be beneficial to help straighten the canter.

Three-track shoulder-in	Yes, as above.	Yes. Normally collected (Figure 6.8) but can be ridden in other tempos when the horse is well trained.	No, not generally used, the canter shoulder-fore being preferred, this exercise being too extreme and if ridden badly (which is easy to do because it is a difficult exercise to ride well) it undoes the good work of the shoulder-in of establishing stability in the horse's shoulders, and inside leg to outside rein. It also has a tendency to put too much strain on the horse's limbs. (Use canter shoulder-fore if you want to try this exercise, but even then you will need a trainer to guide you.) Be *very cautious* about canter shoulder-in. Never do it unless you are experienced or under the instruction of an experienced trainer
Position renvers to shoulder-fore	Yes	Yes	Yes
Renvers	Yes	Yes	Yes, but reserved for advanced horses.

N.B: When the walk and trot is established in the shoulder-fore the rider can begin canter shoulder-fore, but it is best left to knowledgeable riders and under supervision of a trainer. If this exercise is performed the following must be established.

1. Your seat is established; you can ride sitting trot without restricting the forwardness of the horse and you have a good canter seat.

2. The horse must understand the half-halt, be able to engage his hind legs, and be fluid in collected canter work.

3. The canter must already have been made straight by other dressage exercises such as counter-canter and figure riding.

The following set of photos shows and compares various lateral movements performed by horses at different levels (Figures 6.9–6.12).

Figure 6.8   This horse is moving in collected trot shoulder-in showing good carriage, angle and bend.

Figure 6.9   Vicki Thompson riding a near perfect shoulder-in on Jazz Dancer when he was a young horse.

Figure 6.10 A student of the international trainer Bert Rutten working her young horse in shoulder-in and half-pass.

Figure 6.11 Vicki Thompson riding a four-track travers along the track, and when this is compared to Jane Bredin's half-pass you will see that the latter is in fact a travers across the diagonal, four-track travers and half-pass being closely related.

Figure 6.12 International rider Jane Bredin riding a working half-pass on her Grand Prix horse, Cupido. Jane is focusing on improving bend and allowing the hindquarters to lead the forehand slightly as a training exercise for this particular horse.

Suppling the Quarters

Having discovered the purpose of suppling the shoulders let us now look at the benefits of suppling the quarters. There is a risk of over-suppling the horse if the stable base of being able to position the shoulders in front of the quarters has not been established, enabling him to wriggle off the aids. It can present a risk of undoing the straightness of the horse but to avoid this happening, follow the principle of riding the horse forward and straight – a dressage principle that should be imprinted on your mind – then supple the shoulders as explained in the previous section of this chapter, and then you are ready to start lateral work that supples the quarters.

Once this straightness has been achieved, the two main suppling-the-quarters exercises of travers and half-pass can be started. In fact, travers ridden on four tracks with lots of bend is a half-pass, but the work should always be started simply by asking for a little bend and just a good response of the quarters moving away from the outside leg. This response will have been taught through reversed shoulder-in and perhaps simple walk pirouettes on the square. These pirouettes on the square are the exception to the rule about suppling the quarters early in the training (the exercise is detailed on page 230) but they can also be left until travers is started.

Now comes the test of more accuracy, the horse uses different muscles in travers from those he uses in reversed shoulder-in; with travers he is looking in the direction he is moving and therefore shows bend to that direction, and the effect of this movement is to strengthen the muscles through the body, from the outside hind leg to the inside foreleg for example. The horse looks in the direction of movement, and this action builds up the muscles behind the saddle and along the quarters. In other words, these exercises muscle up the horse behind the saddle making his engine more powerful – certainly a bonus for any dressage horse.

Classically, the progression of lateral work goes shoulder-in, travers, renvers, and half-pass, walk pirouettes and canter pirouettes. The quarter pirouettes on the square are a modern exercise and are neither followed by the classical school nor seen in competition, however it is a useful exercise if used with discretion.

This guideline alters to stay flexible to the needs of the horse. It is, however, easier to ride shoulder-in keeping the balance and good bend than to keep the balance showing good bend in travers, and it is easier to keep control of the shoulders of the horse while he moves in travers than if he is moving in half-pass, and for these reasons it is safer to do the suppling exercises in this order:

1.   shoulder-in exercises including all leg-yield work;
2.   walk quarter pirouettes on the square;
3.   travers exercises including all position travers exercises without bend through the body;
4.   renvers exercises emphasizing the simple beginning exercises outlined in this chapter;
5.   half-pass exercises focusing on simple basic half-pass work such as the teardrop half-pass;
6.   walk pirouettes adding several more steps to the quarter pirouette to complete a half circle and progressing to the classical ideal.

(**N.B.** the advanced canter-pirouette work is not covered in this book but it is prepared for by good shoulder-in, travers and half-pass work; these exercises being the foundation of the canter half pass).

As stated, the exception to this rule is the exercise of walk pirouettes on the square that can be started early in the work or left until travers is begun. However, it is not a classically accepted exercise and comes from the Swedish School. Having suppled your horse well through leg-yielding exercises and having dispensed with their use unless a specific reason presents itself (e.g. helping to teach bend through leg-yield across the arena then into half-pass) you should have progressed to the prescribed and accepted ways of riding lateral work.

TRAVERS (QUARTERS-IN)

The first aim of teaching travers is that the horse moves off the outside leg aids, and the second is to teach him inside bend combined with activity forwards and inside bend (Figure 6.13). As stated the horse has already been taught to respond well to the outside leg aids through reversed leg-yield/shoulder-in exercises, reversed shoulder-in and basic walk pirouettes on the square. Always utilize the latter exercise later in the work to avoid confusion, also in dressage shoulder-in takes priority following the principle of shoulders in front of the quarters for active forward movement and straightness.

We start travers by teaching a forward/ sideways response to the outside leg showing

Figure 6.13   The very beginning of travers with a horse just starting the exercise; he shows bend in the head and neck, response to the outside leg, is moving in three tracks and has no bend through the body. Once the horse is suppled through other exercises, bend through the body will come.

very little inside bend, or even no bend at all. Few horses will struggle with this new movement if the preliminary suppling-of-the-shoulders movements have been well taught. Remove the snag of showing good bend by boiling travers down into the following.

1. Response to the outside leg to move the quarters inside the track.
2. Keeping the shoulders along the track at a 30 degree angle while keeping the regularity of the gait and increasing the degree of the angle if the horse comes off the outside rein combined with half-halts on the outside rein, and/or to improve the movement off the outside leg aids.
3. Improving inside bend by teaching greater bend through the corner before travers begins.
4. Keeping the angle and bend the same on both reins before we increase both so that the muscles are developed equally through the body.

Travers is a wonderful exercise when combined with shoulder-in, and prepares for the half-pass, the pinnacle of expression of the horse moving sideways with bend.

WALKING THE SQUARE

This is a basic exercise that can be started early with a young horse, for example, who has undergone the initial stages of training and understands the three gaits moving forwards from the leg and shows a reasonable acceptance of the bridle with contact established to an acceptable degree of proficiency, i.e. he has completed the first 3–6 months of training. It is done in walk, because at each corner of the square the horse does a simple pirouette, and although it can only be done in walk, canter and piaffe, canter pirouette and piaffe pirouette are obviously reserved for advanced dressage horses.

Come into the middle of the arena and visualize a small square slightly bigger than a 10 m circle. This exercise should be ridden in medium walk and you start by riding the first straight side of the square. When you approach the first corner the priority is to get a response to the outside leg but, because this is a novice exercise, the leg is used on, or slightly in front of, the girth in a tap-tap way that asks the horse to move sideways off this leg. At the same time weight your inside seat bone, keeping your inside leg relaxed, and reinforce the outside leg aids with nudges on the outside of the withers with the knuckles. A young horse soon picks up that he gets round each corner of the square by moving his forehand round to the next line he sees.

If you find that you don't get a reaction, check that you are sitting correctly and that your hips and shoulders mirror those of the horse as he makes this turn for the quarter pirouette.

Obviously, this is a basic exercise but it teaches the beginnings of walk pirouette to horse and rider. The horse finds it easy, but you might find the mixture of co-ordination needed presents difficulties until you are well-practised at it.

Perform the exercise a few times and to a maximum of a few minutes on each rein, and when the horse is comfortable with it you can do square-shaped walk serpentines to add interest to the work.

HALF-PASS

This exercise is excellent for suppling the quarters. The movement was developed to help cavalry riders at war: the horse was ridden forward straight followed by traversing away from the enemy, catching them off guard, and we see these exercises in prints of the fifteenth, sixteenth and seventeenth centuries. (The traverse is a manoeuvre that broadly mirrors the modern half-pass.) The ultimate half-pass is the pirouette, which gave the cavalryman a means to move away from the enemy in a line he would not be expecting, a complete turn about: forward straight, circle round, and retreat. These movements were strung together to give the cavalryman a host of attacking positions to attack, to outwit, and to defend. They prepared the horse and rider for battle.

During peace time the riders used their equitation skills in elaborate displays to show off the prowess of the horse and rider to impress the ladies at parties, balls, and charity functions. These displays of artistic riding were performed in riding halls hung with great chandeliers and lit by thousands of candles. In time it became evident that war manoeuvres were excellent for strengthening the muscles of the horse, besides giving the rider greater control, and the movements evolved into a type of stylised ballet we now call dressage.

The half-pass stands out as a beautiful exercise, awesome to watch, but where do we start? Begin with the blueprint, that is half-pass is forward movement with bend. When to start teaching this exercise depends on individual skills and experience. It can be taught early (if the horse knows basic leg-yield/shoulder-in exercises, for example) if you know how to ride it, or have a competent trainer on the ground to help you, otherwise it is best to begin after the other lateral exercises have been taught. Half-pass requires good rider coordination.

Start in walk as you did with suppling the shoulders, but you can progress to rising-trot half-pass quickly; stay in rising trot for five minutes or so before going into sitting trot but do not worry if you prefer to stay in rising trot throughout the whole half-pass exercise because it helps equalize the way the horse uses his diagonals in the trot; this benefit is marked in rising-trot half-pass. But do remember that usually half-pass is ridden in sitting trot for training purposes and always for competitions. The following are the three basic ways to ride it.

Half-pass by the track

Make sure you are comfortable with the leg-yield-parallel-to-the-track exercise. Once this is achieved, ride in a straight line parallel to the long side of the track and ask for a small amount of bend to the side facing the wall. This position in relation to the track can be three steps to the inside to start with but increases until you are positioned parallel to the track along the ¼ and ½ lines and lastly along the centre line. Use your new outside leg 2–4 in (5–10 cm) behind the girth, relax your new inside leg and put your weight onto the inside stirrup. Keep the horse's body parallel to the track to start with. You may find he can show little bend, but providing he is not looking away from the direction in which he is moving this is fine initially. Look at the point on the track at which you want to finish the exercise (this will be the quarter marker), and press and release with your outside leg. If he is resistant to the leg, soften on the outside rein, and sit a little onto the outside seat bone to get him to respond to a half-halt on the outside rein so that he moves his quarters over to finish the exercise neatly. Also check that your shoulders are parallel to the horse's shoulders; this will mean bringing your outside shoulder and hip back a little (Figure 6.14). The first priority must be that the horse is happy to go forward and sideways looking in the direction in which he is moving, the positioning coming from the outside leg. You may find that he is only able to do a handful of strides without losing balance but this is fine. You may also discover that he finds this exercise easier in a brisk trot, so try this and see.

The teardrop half-pass

This is a basic half-pass that moves on three tracks and is the half-pass normally asked for in Medium-level competition (Figures 6.15a–c). At this stage the horse should find it easy to show good bend on a three-track half-pass, whereas at the more advanced levels he will be expected to show a lot more bend and travel on four tracks. Remember that the amount of bend shows the amount of suppleness through his body, and if we ask for too much bend before he is ready this makes the half-pass a leg-yield type of movement. To help understand the difference we can also compare the three-track travers with the four-track travers, the latter being more advanced with the horse showing a much greater degree of bend through the body; the four-track travers is really a half-pass along the track.

You want to encourage the horse to show a little more inside bend. Let us assume you are riding on the left rein; slowly ask for more inside bend with a

Figure 6.14   The first stages of teaching half-pass in trot (travelling from the $^1/_4$ line track to the outside track). You can see the stability of the outside leg and the rider sitting with her outside shoulder back and inside shoulder a little forward. She has more weight on the outside seat bone, but once inside bend moving forwards into the half-pass is established she will have more weight on the inside seat bone, still keeping the same position with the outside of her body.

Figures 6.15a –c   A first lesson in half-pass is on a teardrop shape. a) Quarters leading. b) The shoulders should lead to ensure forwardness, but here the shoulders lead a tad too much. c) This rear view of half-pass shows a good angle and the shoulders are leading, which is good.

relaxed inside leg (not too far behind the girth because this will stop inside bend), and sit further round to the increased bend you are asking for (i.e. 1–2 in [2.5–5 cm] maximum) but your left hip should be a little more forward to allow for this increase in bend. Ask for this increase as you come around the arc of the corner (the middle of the corner) and increase it slightly as you come into the half circle of the teardrop shape. Once you have ridden around the half circle you will take a diagonal line back to the quarter marker but you still keep inside bend. In lateral work the bend is in the direction in which the horse is moving, except with leg-yield and shoulder-in. I mention this so that you are not confused: for left half-pass the horse moves with left bend along the diagonal line back to the track and the inside bend is on the left side. The outside of the horse is the right side which, because you have technically changed the rein, would under normal circumstances be the inside. It is simple if you remember that the inside leg asks for forward movement and bend, and the outside leg asks for the sideways movement and is positioned behind the girth. Half-pass is forward sideways showing bend.

The zig-zag

This form of the half-pass is ridden in a zig-zag shape when the horse moves back and forth over a straight line. Normally the zig-zag is ridden over the centre line and at the levels discussed in this book it is ridden in walk and trot and in collected trot for the lower levels of competition.

You use exactly the same riding aids as for the other half-passes, the only difference being that you straighten the horse for one stride before positioning the horse for the new direction for the next 'zig' of the zig-zag. You must make sure that there is no swinging of the horse's head from one direction to the other when you ask for the next change of direction and that you have the horse correctly positioned to the new bend with your weight on the new inside seat bone and using your new inside leg. If you follow this rule the movement is easy.

Zig-zags are normally performed in numbers of steps. For example: 3 half-pass steps to the left, 6 to the right, 6 to the left, 6 to the right, completing the exercise with three half-pass steps to the left again; or, 4 steps to the left, 8 to the right, 8 to the left, 8 to the right, and 4 to the left to finish the exercise. The movement is started at D or G on the centre line and finished at D or G, depending on in which direction you are moving.

Zig-zags are good for fine-tuning the half-pass once the basics are well established and are best started in walk and then trot.

Tips on riding half-pass

To begin with horses can find showing good bend in half-pass difficult; they might stiffen and show no bend, or tip the head. To counteract this, ride half-pass with only a little bend and improve softness on the inside bend through shoulder-in work. Often a Medium-level horse will need to return to shoulder-in work in order to perfect the half-pass, because if the bend is not correct the horse will always struggle with half-pass. Using shoulder-ins and leg-yields combined with half-passes helps here.

But let's not get too ahead of ourselves, we have a straighter horse but it will be years before he is straight enough for high levels of collection, and we will discover that he will have a tendency to show more bend on one rein than the other. This depends on the natural suppleness of each horse and the level of training he has received, but it will be a tendency found in every horse first learning half-pass.

When riding half-pass if you think 'inside hip a little forward' you discover that you do not need to move the outside leg too far behind the girth and this keeps the power in your seat. The further the leg is positioned behind the line of your hip to heel the more you compromise your balance in the saddle, the effectiveness of the leg aids can be lost and stronger leg aids need to be used. This is the opposite of what you want.

The horse does not understand the aids of the outside leg as easily as those of the inside one unless he is truly on the outside rein but by teaching him to react well to the outside leg aids you not only prepare him for travers and half-pass but also increase the training potential for his acceptance of the outside rein. This, in effect, improves straightness. To start these exercises you may exaggerate the outside leg aid by positioning the leg further back, but once the horse gets going in this work it can be positioned further forward. There are always exceptions to this rule. Try to find each horse's 'button', i.e. the place behind the girth that suits him, and position the outside leg there. I find that big-moving horses, or those with long backs, need the leg further back behind the girth, whereas mares and sensitive breeds such as the Thoroughbred only need the leg placed a few inches behind the girth otherwise the outside leg seems to irritate them and they get very upset by it. The best advice is to be sensitive to each horse's preferences so that you do not cause counter reactions which will then need to be corrected.

Sit with your shoulder and hips level. The inside leg is kept relaxed, and there should be more weight on the inside stirrup. Do not put too much inside leg on or the horse will get confused and will not move off the outside leg, and the half-pass is stopped. Weight on the inside seat bone gives the leg aid – the seat bones are the leg aids because, as any classical rider will testify, they are the top of the leg and are closer to the horse's centre of gravity than the legs themselves. In dressage less equals more, and when you use your seat bones in a coordinated way you get more results with less effort and with the chances of counter reactions from the horse being minimized. If a horse is sticky moving off the outside leg, place more weight on the outside seat bone, and if there is still no reaction soften the outside rein without pulling but by a gentle closing of the fingers. Never pull back towards the hips but always soften through the elbows first (¼–½ in [approximately 1 cm]) and then return the arms to their original position and soften without losing the bend and without dropping the rein.

The rein on which the horse shows more bend you may need to keep more outside rein to lessen the chances of the horse hanging on the inside rein or to counteract any stiffness and/or hollowing. This brings the hindquarters over off the outside leg aids and prevents the horse's neck bending too much to the inside caused by too much bend through this side of the body. On a horse's stiffer rein, which tends to be the right rein, you need to coax bend on this stiffer side by making sure that your outside shoulder is relaxed, your outside elbow is soft, and you give a little on the outside rein to position the horse to the inside. To encourage this acceptance of the outside rein when it is the stiffer rein, take the inside bend, and then reconnect with the outside rein, because this allows connection to the rein the horse favours, while allowing you to check the softness of your elbows and hands on the side of your body corresponding to the horse's stiffer side so that when you make the reconnection to the outside rein through a gentle half-halt, there should be a better reaction from the horse.

However, these actions will often not be necessary because if you sit well for the movement you will find it happens naturally without these corrections. You must be sure that on the hollow side, usually the left rein, you have an elastic contact on the outside rein, but you must also have a contact on the inside rein, because the horse will try to drop the inside contact on the hollow side, i.e. the left rein if the horse is hollow to the left and stiff to the right.

When the horse moves sideways easily in half-pass and understands the aids you can begin to use the inside bend and forward leg aids for riding the half-pass with the aids coordinated in the classical way of riding, i.e. the inside leg asks for bend and forward movement and is positioned on the girth or slightly in front of it; the outside leg asks for the sideways movement and controls the outside hind leg. The inside hand asks for inside bend and the outside hand keeps a consistent outside contact. But once the half-pass is established, the corrections described are not necessary; the rider applies the aids, sits for the movement and rides it forwards as a forward movement with bend encouraging better bend and activity.

Keep the movement in walk and trot until it is well-established, then you can begin the canter half-pass, which presents no problem once the trot half-pass is good.

7 SECOND NATURE

DRESSAGE BECOMES SECOND nature when training is combined with good practice. The rider progresses proactively and results happen in a natural easy way. This brings confidence and as you grow in confidence you feel happy which, in turn, prompts you to learn more. Fired with more enthusiasm these healthy responses initiate a positive circle of learning. The following points are new ways to fine-tune your learning progress and develop confidence even further.

- Develop an eye for dressage by watching good competition and trainers teaching dressage that you consider applies to specific exercises that will help you.
- Have more lessons covering areas in which you particularly wish to progress.
- Ride more horses.
- Prepare horses for dressage competitions and compete.
- Attend demonstrations and clinics.
- Get involved in judging or writing for judges at dressage competitions.
- Study books and videos.
- Consolidate areas of riding that need improvement.

Once you have developed a good riding position, and have practised dressage exercises correctly, you will ride on automatic pilot, yet you may want to push out the boundaries and go even further. There are no rules, only the measure of your desire to learn and train and go forward in the way that suits you. You develop an eye for dressage by being immersed in it, and this enriches the quality of your riding.

Trainability

'The horse can do dressage without the rider, but can the rider do dressage without the horse?' This saying comes from the Spanish Riding School of Vienna. We need to learn humility before we can train a horse in a way that does him justice, and only through this humility will we be open to being taught in a way that allows us to progress well. Only by being teachable can we learn from others, and only by being taught will we be able to teach the horse. We work with nature not against it and we are disciplined to control negative reactions, for example we behave in a proactive way and do not respond to situations in a reactive negative way. If we follow these guidelines dressage teaches us many truths about everyday living.

We cannot *make* the horse do anything because he is stronger and quicker than us, and when we appreciate this fact it brings us down to earth in a way that transcends the ordinary and does not cause difficulties or hardships in our lives but gives a boost to our life experiences. The crunch comes when we ride to train a horse because actively schooling the horse whenever we ride, and not just riding him passively, prompts thinking and responsible attitudes that can widen our appreciation of the horse besides equipping us with assets beyond our imagination. For example, I know of top yards where hundreds of thousands of pounds are paid for expensive dressage horses, yet the results are poor, the horses' abilities not reflecting the money invested. Good dressage horses come from good dressage riding and this requires a positive, thinking-riding approach. The rewards are there if you want to take them and are prepared to work towards them, and part of this learning process is looking beyond the normal learning ways.

With regard to the horse: his trainability is demonstrated in his willingness to learn, to be moulded in the way we want him to go according to his talents,

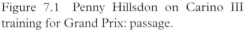

Figure 7.1 Penny Hillsdon on Carino III training for Grand Prix: passage.

Figure 7.2 Penny Hillsdon on Carino III training for Grand Prix: working trot.

conformation, and character. Average horses can outdo a top-flight horse if they are well ridden and have been well trained. This opens opportunities to riders who cannot afford expensive horses. There have been Olympic medallists who have ridden inexpensive horses; for example I know of one horse who was bought off the racetrack for $350, and another, a warmblood, bought for £2,600 – both became Olympic dressage horse. The aspiring rider need not be disillusioned by big swanky horseboxes, or super-duper horses that perform dressage coming out the womb. Remember, **dressage is about training**. Good dressage training gets results.

Assessing the Horse and Rider

These assessments provide information that can be acted upon to give direction for your training. You need to know the goal you are aiming towards in the same way as the traveller needs a road map to reach a destination. It is practically impossible to get where you want to go without knowing where you are going!

The horse assessment is best done at six-month intervals and usually takes place during a lesson, whereas the rider assessment is more of a sports profile and is usually done sitting down with your trainer having a cup of coffee and a talk. Both types of assessment identify the present situations, consider future aims, and discuss potential future results from following a good training programme.

THE HORSE ASSESSMENT

With this assessment the emphasis is on the horse although the rider's input is considered, for example the marks for the Rider Position encourage you to think about the effects your riding position is having on the horse's way of going, not by being negative about your riding skills but by being positive about you and your horse. To assess the horse the trainer asks you to show the three gaits of walk, trot and canter on both reins, and any other work you want to show. You will assess the horse together afterwards and award marks from 1–10 as if riding a competition. Take your time riding the exercise, there is no rush because it is an informal exercise to encourage future training, but normally it takes approximately 20 minutes. In the post-exercise rider and

trainer discussion, the rider may give marks for a few points, and the trainer for others, but they both agree on the marks given. Disagreement is rare but if it does happen it is good for rider and trainer to discuss their different viewpoints and perceptions, to keep an open mind, listen to each

Figure 7.3 Angela and Only a Question of Time placed 4th on 70.36% in their first major dressage competition.

other's opinions and come to an agreement over the marking. The marks are generous to encourage the rider but also realistic, and the trainer will outline the direction training should take to get the assessment marks for six months time.

Riders are often daunted by having to ride a horse for this assessment, but rather they should be confident and encouraged. Once it is finished they realize it is a useful exercise and not difficult. The trainer makes the comments and marks out of ten in a notebook and can either keep them or give them to the rider. They are often used for reference for future assessments. Below is a typical initial assessment; the next assessment will show the original marks so that they can be compared.

NAME OF HORSE		
Assessment points	**Marks now (Date)**	**Marks for six months**
The gaits (focusing on rhythm, spring and throughness) as below		
Trot	6	7.5
Canter	6	6.5
Walk	6	7
Contact	5.5	7
Trainability	7	7.5
Rider position	6.5	7
Other areas (e.g. lateral work if applicable, or other movements)		

THE RIDER'S SPORTS PROFILE

This assessment covers areas like: feel for rhythm, co-ordination ability, concentration, ability to ride using intelligence and technique rather than reacting to situations, rider position, competition results and future aspirations, the team helping the rider, future goals and the best way to get help to achieve them; in fact any areas trainer and rider consider need to be discussed so that future aims can be achieved. For example, teamwork is something that can open up unthought-of opportunities. After a discussion a short report is typed up and presented to the rider.

Often the results bring great benefits. You may realize that if you had not discussed a particular point during the profile, you might never have achieved a goal. Confidence grows. It is a wonderful feeling to know that you are part of a team and not on your own. This is the purpose of the sports profile.

Talent

To ride dressage well you need different forms of talent: a good sense of balance, good rhythm, a willingness to learn, the ability to persevere, physical attributes that allow you to improve your seat and position your body (i.e. muscle tone) a natural ability with animals, and a mind that can accumulate knowledge yet put it into practice. Often a rider will excel in some areas of dressage riding but need to work harder to overcome limitations in others. Few riders lack talents, it is just a matter of discovering them and, once they are found, improving them, and drawing upon them in every riding situation. Talent is God given, yet we must work at it to fulfil it.

Flattering students can put pressure on them, and so it is best avoided, but gentle encouragement on a regular basis is far more sensible. It is better that a rider works steadily and builds upon talents rather than relying on them, otherwise she will never be able to identify her weaknesses and win the deep-down character-building benefits of dressage. There is something about dressage training that gets the poisons out of the system, that slays the dragons, it is as if the horse gives us a mystical way to deeper understanding of the human race.

Figure 7.4   My rather large warmblood and I compete in our first Medium unaffiliated competition at Windsor where we came 2nd.

Figure 7.5   Dressage boosts your edge in all competitions; in their first cross-country competition, Tina and Arrow came 5th out of 55.

The horse helps the rider, and the rider helps the horse – dressage is a two-way relationship. Once this is achieved, the work to bring out the polish can be added. A talented horse still needs to be trained gradually, and correctly, it must not be rushed. It is like polishing a wooden table; with careful and consistent polishing a gorgeous sheen comes that shows off the grain of the wood, but if it is rubbed or scuffed the sheen goes. If you rely solely on natural talent to train, you score the wood with a knife, and the polish deepens the cut. The only way to correct this fault is to strip the polish off and start again. It is important not to take advantage of natural talents with dressage training. Horses and people with talent can be temperamental, and rushing aggravates the character rather than enhances it. A rider proceeds with care and consideration and a trainer nurses her students keeping them grounded in the principles of dressage training.

The Power of Dressage

Riding dressage can be full of surprises. We learn more about ourselves, we come closer to the horse and along the training route we discover inner depths to our characters. It is no surprise that we see T-shirts emblazoned with, 'Love me love my horse.' Such maxims give clues that riding is special and dressage magnifies the special qualities. Neither is it a surprise that Jilly Cooper has had such success writing about the lives of riders. There is between horse and rider something romantic, something thrilling, which makes this a unique activity. Dressage riding is down-to-earth, earthier than any other form of riding (earthy but sensual, practical yet artistic) and the rider has a closeness with the horse that distinguishes it from the ordinary.

The dressage rider focuses on quality – 'quality' is the motto – yet without being a prima donna. The training fosters polite attitudes, a consideration for others, consideration between horse and rider. This politeness is expressed in other forms such as following the right etiquette for the right occasion and being respectful of others feelings and it brings a sense of beauty.

Dressage is powerful, sometimes a cure for the ills of modern life, but the rider is wise to take the right medicine in the right doses. I have often observed how training acts like a poultice drawing out the poisons from a person's personality. Something remarkable, something mystical, seems to happen, demons are killed in the process of dressage riding and the hero hidden within us is released. We become bold and beautiful, ready to take on the world together – rider and horse. The freedom of expression displayed in the horse's gaits, the freedom of the rider's abilities lighting afresh the flame of the unique relationship between man and beast; this is dressage riding.

One more word of encouragement to help you towards better dressage: 'Smile, you're riding dressage.' Never let it be said that you don't give it your best shot, then you can experience instant freedom from the greyness of everyday life and move into a realm of special moments of you and your horse working in harmony.

Figure 7.6 Something mystical happens when we ride dressage, the hero in us is brought out.

INDEX